10901662

STEAMBOATS IN DAKOTA TERRITORY

STEAMBOATS IN DAKOTA TERRITORY

Transforming the Northern Plains

TRACY POTTER

THE History PRESS

Published by The History Press
Charleston, SC
www.historypress.net

Copyright © 2017 by Tracy Potter
All rights reserved

Front cover: *The Steamboat* Yellow Stone *Arriving Fort Union Trading Post, circa 1835*, by Robert Back. *Courtesy Lord John Jacob Astor of Hever and Darrell Dorgan.*

Back cover, top: Drawing of the sternwheel packet *Far West. Courtesy Special Collections, Murphy Library, University of Wisconsin-La Crosse*; *center-right*: Sitting Bull, Tatanka Iyatake. *Courtesy Fort Abraham Lincoln Foundation.*

First published 2017

Manufactured in the United States

ISBN 9781467119344

Library of Congress Control Number: 2017934937

Notice: The information in this book is true and complete to the best of our knowledge. It is offered without guarantee on the part of the author or The History Press. The author and The History Press disclaim all liability in connection with the use of this book.

All rights reserved. No part of this book may be reproduced or transmitted in any form whatsoever without prior written permission from the publisher except in the case of brief quotations embodied in critical articles and reviews.

Blessed are the peacemakers, in every culture, in every time.

CONTENTS

Contents

ACKNOWLEDGEMENTS

In the acknowledgements to *Sheheke: Mandan Indian Diplomat*, I credited my interest in history to individuals who stoked that interest. I failed to credit the excellent public school education my generation of North Dakotans received, virtually free of cost from kindergarten through graduate school, and the nonstructured time children of my age were allowed so we could investigate and develop our interests. Thanks, Andrew Carnegie, for the library.

Now, as an unstructured person of my age, I need to acknowledge Franklin Delano Roosevelt for Social Security. Thanks, FDR, for the time.

More directly, thank you, Greg Dumais, for reaching out from Charleston and The History Press to enquire if I would like to write a book for the company. The answer was yes. Edward Mack, Chad Rhoad and Julia Turner have followed through as helpful editorial contacts.

The Fort Abraham Lincoln Foundation started me down the path of researching and writing about steamboats as part of a project to bring a new historical facility to the Port of Bismarck, where the foundation operates the *Lewis and Clark* riverboat on the Missouri. Its photograph files, including some 1926 glass plate positives, helped illustrate the book, thanks to Aaron Barth and Diane Warner. The foundation's library and the North Dakota State Library had all the secondary sources needed. Laura Gooden of Murphy Library Special Collections, University of Wisconsin–La Crosse, helped with illustrations. Jim Davis of the State Historical Society of North Dakota Archives, helped with research, and his co-worker Sarah Walker provided most of the other illustrations.

Acknowledgements

Dr. William E. Lass is the dean of Missouri River transportation scholars. His works are encyclopedic and an essential reference source. Mike Casler of Williston knows more about steamboats in Dakota and Fort Union than I ever will and is willing to share that information. Every historian relies on the work of other historians for context and detail. At any moment while writing this book, there were two dozen other books surrounding me, literally, with sticky notes or grocery coupons or envelopes marking passages. I thank the impulse that makes people research and write history.

Searching for appropriate cover art, I thought of two great pieces of art I knew involving steamboat stories within the book: *Far West: Custer at the Rosebud*, a detailed close-up of a moment in history by Robert Sticker, and Gary Miller's lovely *Silent Wheel*, an image of the *F.Y. Batchelor* stuck in ice. Sam McQuade gave me permission to use his original of Miller's work, and Miller's widow, Darla, was gracious as well. One bothersome note was that both images were of events that took place in Montana. Then I saw *The Steamboat* Yellowstone *Arriving Fort Union Trading Post, c. 1835*. In this painting, commissioned by Lord John Jacob Astor of Hever, Robert Back said just about everything I intended to say in a book. And it happened in Dakota Territory. Through Parliamentary Assistant Tracy Murrell, Lord Hever granted his permission to use it, and as serendipity would have it, my neighbor and friend Darrell Dorgan owned the artist's proof.

INTRODUCTION

The Missouri River is North America's longest. From the Rockies to the Gulf of Mexico, it runs nearly four thousand miles and drains more than one-third of the forty-eight contiguous states. Although it loses its name after meeting the Mississippi by St. Charles, Missouri, it shouldn't. The description of Father Charlevoix in 1721 shows why: "The two rivers are much the same breadth, each about half a league; but the Missouri is by far the most rapid, and seems to enter the Mississippi like a conqueror, through which it carries its white waters to the opposite shore without mixing them, after wards, it gives its color to the Mississippi which it never loses again but carries quite down to the sea."[1]

The Missouri was called *Mat'tah* by the Mandan and *Mni Sose* by the Lakota. The Arikara said *Tswaarúxti* and the Hidatsa *Awati*. From the Illinois Indians to people along its banks today, it has been known as Muddy or the Big Muddy. It is named for one of the many nations that lived along its banks, the Missouris or Missouria, who knew themselves as *Niúachi*. In the 1600s, they lived in Dakota, along the Missouri at the point where the Grand River enters. The Bureau of American Ethnology says the name *Missouri* has nothing to do with mud but references "town of wooden lodges." Those were earthlodges, a house type the Niúachi had in common with the Arikara, Mandan and Hidatsa of Dakota.

An explorer and fur trader from New France came to the Missouri in Dakota in 1738 without knowing it was the same river Charlevoix had seen at its mouth, eight hundred miles downriver. Pierre Gaultier de Varennes,

Sieur de la Verendrye, thought he might be the first non-Indian to see what he called the River of the West. He hoped it would lead to the Sea of the West. It didn't. It led to the Gulf of Mexico and thus to the Atlantic Ocean. La Verendrye was indeed the first non-Indian to see the Red River of the North. It led to the same known sea, though by a different route, through Hudson Bay and on to the Atlantic. He built a fort there at the meeting of the Red and the Assiniboine Rivers, a place where Winnipeg grew.

La Verendrye visited the earthlodge people, known to him as *Mantannes*, in what is now central North Dakota. Within a few years, the confusion was settled as La Verendrye's sons made a roundabout trip from the *Mantannes* to Wyoming and back to the Dakotas, where they were hosted by Arikara Indians on the banks of the Missouri near what became the capital of South Dakota. By the time they traveled back north, they knew where the river flowed. What they still didn't know was whence it came. It would be many decades before the source of the Missouri was known to the world's mapmakers.

Perhaps counterintuitively, native peoples did not much use the Missouri for transportation. Canoes were, apparently, rare on the Missouri in what became Dakota. Bull boats were more usual. Made with willow frames covered by buffalo hides, these round vessels could carry several passengers or a few hundred pounds of meat. In the relatively swift current of the Missouri, bull boats would drift downriver faster than they could be paddled across it, making it necessary to walk upstream a quarter mile or so to end up on the other bank opposite to where they started.

The first canoes and pirogues in Dakota seem to have come with traders of French descent paddling up from St. Louis in the 1790s. Lewis and Clark followed in their wake on a fifty-six-foot-long keelboat in 1804. They dug out pirogues for their return trip. In the decades following, other keelboats went upriver and down, and in 1825, an experiment converted keelboats into wheel boats, powered by the crewmen. Rather than pulling on oars, the crew's labor turned paddlewheels on each side of keelboat. It worked well enough to be used by an armada carrying treaties to tribes in the Dakotas. After some fits and starts, a steamboat first chugged against the current of the Missouri and into Dakota in 1831, twenty-four years after Fulton's Folly demonstrated the practicality of steamboats for river traffic on the Hudson in New York.

Steamboats' speed and power transformed a region and forever affected relations between the United States and the several Indian nations of Dakota. Every attempt to climb "the spiral staircase to the Rockies" had to consider the difficulties of ice, snags, sawyers, sandbars and low water. It was noticed that there were two rises in the river each year. The first was during spring in the valley, when creeks and ravines filled with snowmelt and spring rains and the water worked its way, via the Missouri, to the Gulf of Mexico. The second came in June with snowmelt in the mountains. Getting boats upriver depended on those rises, and steamboats could much better take advantage of them simply by being faster going upstream. They could linger longer into August or September because they raced downstream faster than the river dropped or froze.

Steamboats changed relations with the Indian nations of Dakota: the Assiniboine, Crow, Hidatsa, Mandan, Arikara, Ojibway, Cheyenne, Hunkpapa, Brulé, Oglalla, Sans Arc, Teton, Yankton and Yanktonnai. Along the Red River, they affected the Metís of Pembina. Steamboats provided a distinct and overt technological advantage to the Americans. They carried very large loads—of trade goods, men, guns and cannon. They were impressive, useful and an object of considerable skepticism among the Indians.

Buffalo robes, beaver, mink, muskrat and manufactured art and clothing flowed down to profit merchants in St. Louis, New York, London and Leipzig, while guns, powder and shot, mirrors, metal tools and European beads traveled the other direction. The trade was mutually beneficial, though often disputed by intertribal competition. An inevitable arms race led to downstream nations opposing traders going beyond them. Being the middleman in a trading network is better than being cut out of the trade.

Trade, to the dismay of the Indians, was accompanied by trappers and miners and, eventually, soldiers. Steamboats brought them and supplied them. Steamboats were floating fortresses with pilothouses lined with metal to deflect rifle fire and often soldiers on board, ready to launch campaigns. Between supplying forts and agencies and distributing treaty commodities, private business did very well with government contracts, and the fur trade with Indians retreated in importance to being only a fraction of a fraction of the steamboat business. White trappers and hunters competed even for the fraction that was the robe and fur trade.

Then steamboats became a weapon of war. As the United States clashed repeatedly with the Great Sioux Nation, steamers were contracted for troop movement, supply and scouting. The *Far West* and Grant Marsh were there doing all that and more for the campaign of 1876–77. Marsh was still captaining boats after the campaign, carrying Sioux families to reservations after their surrender, repeating a pattern that steamboats played in removing Indians from southern Minnesota to central Dakota in 1863.

Railroads reached Fargo on the Red River in 1872 and Yankton and Bismarck on the Missouri in 1873. The Panic of 1873 delayed plans to continue the routes west of the Missouri, and those cities grew in importance as cogs in a transportation network, with rails bringing goods and people to their Missouri River ports, where steamboats could distribute them at docks up and down the Missouri and Yellowstone.

The rails that accelerated the Dakota steamboat industry and built ports doomed them, too. There is an observable recurring theme of technological advances and pursuit of short-term profit wrecking the chances for sustainable economies. The deadly voyage of the *St. Peters* up the Missouri in 1837 that killed thousands of customers; delivery of the railroad engine Countess of Dufferin by steamboat to Winnipeg on the Red in 1879, helping railroads replace steamboats; trappers and hunters eliminating their own livelihoods as they emptied streams of beaver and the plains of bison; and countless shipments of rail laborers, equipment and supplies by steamboat to sites up and down the rivers exhibit the short-sightedness that sustains the cliché that a capitalist will sell the rope to his own hanging.

After a railroad bridge crossed the Missouri at Bismarck in 1881, the growing cities directly west along the Yellowstone in Montana were almost immediately connected with Bismarck by rail and reached that way without transshipment long before a steamboat could go northwest to Fort Union and then southwest to Miles City or Billings. Rails continued to cross and then crisscross the region, stitching the communities together. After 1881, the steamboat industry became a niche sector in transportation of farm commodities. It produced profit while steadily declining in importance until it faded away completely, communities along the river observing a series of last landings and departures. H.M. Chittenden was largely correct in writing "The final blow was delivered to the river trade in 1887, when the Great Northern reached Helena."

Steamboats in Dakota were consigned to history. This is one.

Chapter 1

AN ANCIENT MALL OF AMERICA

While glaciers in the last ice age reached into what became Dakota Territory, ice did not entirely cover Dakota. Fifteen thousand years ago, people on the south bank of the Missouri River could see on the other side the massive wall of ice that had turned the course of the river away from Hudson Bay to its modern meeting with the Mississippi. When the glaciers receded, people filled in behind. In the most recent millennium, some people of Dakota maintained a nomadic life, following the plentiful bison. Others developed successful sedentary societies along the Missouri. The groups periodically came together to trade at villages along the river.

Ten thousand years before those villages appeared, a beautiful, translucent brown stone, easily worked, was found by people who hunted mammoths and giant bison on the grassy plains that later became Dunn County, North Dakota. Folsom man, so denoted by his style of tool-making, quarried Knife River flint and knapped it into spear points, scrapers and other tools of the hunter-gatherer lifestyle.

The stone traveled. By two thousand years ago, the flint could be found in New Mexico, South Carolina, Ohio and the Canadian north. In the following thousand years, settlements began springing up along the Missouri River. Obsidian from the Rockies and shells from faraway coasts mix with flint, eagle bone whistles and pottery shards in the archaeological record of the villages of the people who became known to history as the Mandan, Hidatsa and Arikara.

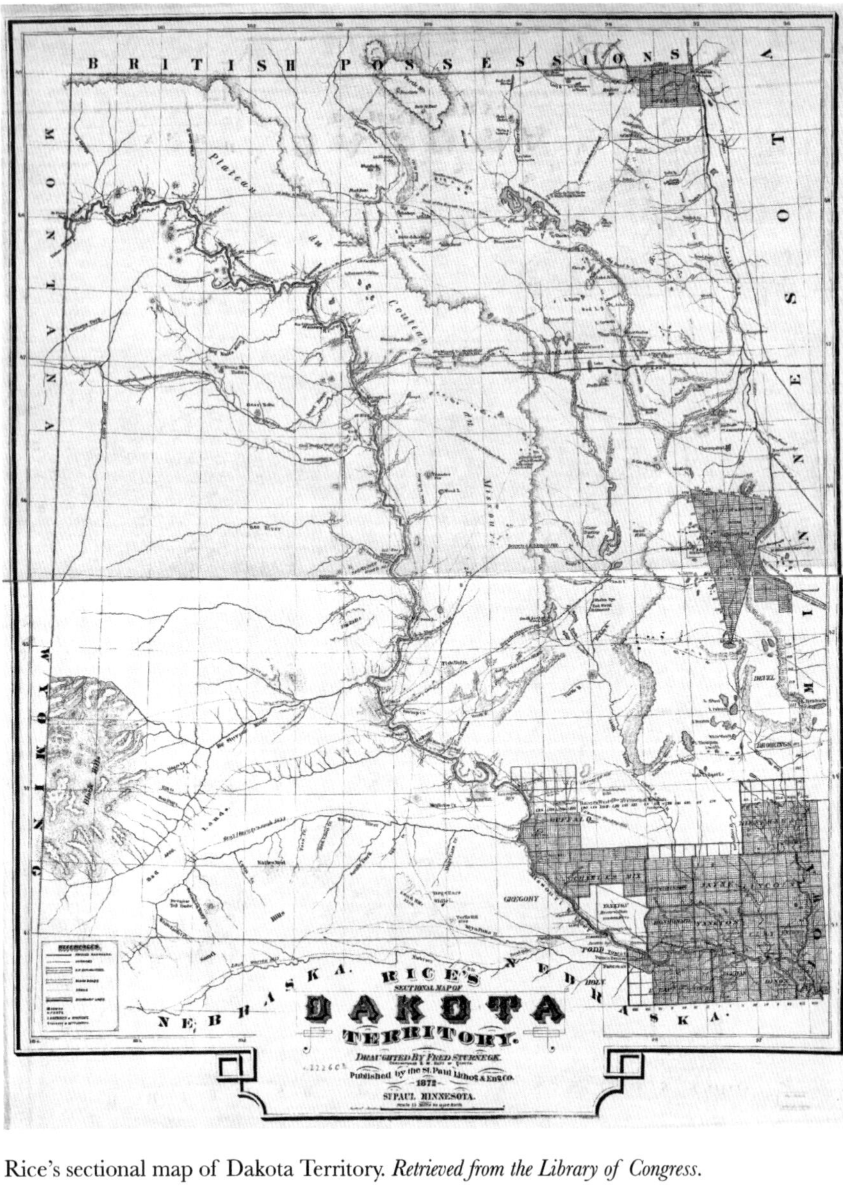

Rice's sectional map of Dakota Territory. *Retrieved from the Library of Congress.*

Those people took up a successful gender-based division of labor, with women farming and men hunting. The farming women successfully adapted strains of corn to the short growing seasons of Dakota and grew many varieties of beans and squash. They learned how to dry and store agricultural surplus. Buffalo, elk, antelope and deer were beyond plentiful on the Dakota plains and balanced the grain and vegetable diet. Food surpluses produced a valuable trade good. Permanent cities with food to trade brought visitors from a wide region.

The prehistoric continent-wide trade network had hubs—settled cities in some regions, a certain rendezvous in others. In the last two centuries before white contact, the settled cities of Dakota were along the Missouri, with the Arikara in the upper half of what became South Dakota and their long-term enemies, the Hidatsa and Mandan, in central North Dakota. Those cities, in the 1700s, were at advantageous spots at the meeting point of the expanding frontiers of guns from the north and east and horses from the south and west. The three tribes found their villages to be profitable places to trade horses for guns and vice versa, gaining from each exchange as the friendly middlemen.

For those peoples, the Missouri River, Grandmother to the Mandan, meant many things, and none of them was transportation. As farmers, they appreciated that the river gave them fertile soils, renewed by regular spring floods. It provided water, food and a place to bathe. They bathed a lot. Food from the river at the breakup of ice in March or April included floating buffalo collected by young men jumping from shore to ice floe and then from one to the other carrying a lariat to tow the bison back to shore. When the distance was too great to leap, the young Mandan would dive into the frigid water, swim to the next floe and pull himself up. They were hardy folk indeed.[2]

The urban Indians on the Missouri were well adapted to their environment and evolved sustainable cities. For three or four hundred years, villages lasted only fifty years or less. Earthlodges require a lot of wood and needed to be rebuilt every ten or so years. The wood resource in Dakota is not abundant, so villages were born and died as the people moved up and down the valley. But sometime around 1500, the Mandan and Hidatsa adopted the Arikara architectural choice of round lodges, requiring fewer logs. Thereafter, some of their cities lasted two or three hundred years, being abandoned only after the smallpox epidemic of 1781.

The 1781 epidemic swept central and western North America. The more nomadic groups tended to have higher survival rates and this affected post-epidemic power in Dakota.

When explorers of European descent began entering the area, the Nakota division of Sioux, the Yankton and Yanktonnai dominated the southeast corner of Dakota. The Seven Council Fires of Lakota Sioux bands, *Oceti Sakowin*, roamed vast regions touching on the Missouri, Hunkpapa farthest

Mounted warriors apparently from a slide show commemorating fiftieth anniversary of the Battle of the Little Big Horn. *Courtesy Fort Abraham Lincoln Foundation.*

north and Oglalla to the south. Brulé, Sans Arc, Miniconjou, Blackfoot and Two Kettles populated the region between. The Lakota were a very loose confederation of many smaller nomadic groups. Arikara Indians had dozens of villages along the Missouri south of what became the border between North Dakota and South Dakota. Above that line were earthlodge villages of the Mandan and Hidatsa. Above the Hidatsa, the Assiniboine hunted.

Chapter 2

ENTER THE EUROPEANS

European trade goods reached the village Indians of the upper Missouri nearly a century and a half before the Europeans themselves. They traveled far along the traditional intertribal trade networks. It took nearly 200 years after Columbus for European traders to get within one thousand miles of the villages. It was 246 years after Columbus's first visit to the Western Hemisphere that a Quebec-born Frenchman was carried into an earthlodge village near the Missouri.

The curiosities from Europe entering the native trade routes included glass beads, metal tools and articles of clothing. Those things fit neatly into tribal culture without altering it. Stone knives, scrapers and awls work just fine, but metal ones were still desired for their durability. Making beads and adorning clothing with quillwork was hard work. Glass beads from Europe caught on as a fashion accessory.

By the 1680s, the English were nine hundred miles away from the earthlodges, sitting at Fort Nelson in western Hudson Bay. Oceangoing ships stopped there to provision the traders at the fort and to haul away profitable furs in exchange for Brazilian tobacco, guns, articles of clothing and Hudson Bay blankets. The Hudson's Bay Company (HBC) sold Hudson Bay blankets on Hudson Bay. The French were at the western end of Lake Superior, at Kaministiqua, just five hundred miles from the Missouri. Their canoes mimicked the work of the sailing ships on Hudson Bay, hauling goods back and forth from the frontier to Quebec, where they could be transferred to ships for crossing the Atlantic. Farther south on the Missouri, St. Louis—

eight hundred miles away from the Mandan villages and the only water route from them to the outside world—wasn't established until 1764.

The French were the first to establish trading posts on the northern plains. They canoed and portaged as far as they could from Quebec and then walked the last couple hundred miles to the Missouri.

The Missouri was the "River of the West," to the French in Canada in the early eighteenth century. They hoped it might lead to the "Sea of the West." That there might exist a Sea of the West that was not the Pacific but was perhaps connected to it was a peculiar and long-held French belief based on information misunderstood by French officials. The Sea of the West's relationship to the Pacific is probably best seen as similar in nature to the way the Mediterranean is connected to the Atlantic, allowing oceangoing vessels to reach far into the space between Europe and Africa.

The Missouri, for a brief time, was two separate rivers to the French. They knew it at and upriver from its confluence with the Mississippi, and they knew it at the earthlodge villages of the people they called *Mantannes.* In the early 1740s, they just didn't know it was the same river. To the distress of their search for the Western Sea, they learned that it was a known river and that going downstream would not help them find the Pacific Ocean.

But upstream there was another treasure. There were fur trade riches to be found in the upper Missouri and its tributaries, particularly the Yellowstone. And upstream, of course, would eventually lie the path of Lewis and Clark and immigrants to the United States taking the "great spiral staircase to the Rockies,"[3] a staircase that rose about 1 foot per mile. It climbed 2,167 feet from St. Louis, 465 feet above sea level, to Fort Benton, in Montana, at 2,632 feet.

While Frenchmen would explore, hunt and trade with the Indian peoples of the Rockies, the nation of France would not be part of the picture after the 1763 Treaty of Paris. With the cessation of hostilities at the close of the French and Indian War, the North American theater of the global Seven Years' War, France surrendered New France and turned over its Canadian colony to England. French king Louis XV had taken steps to preempt Louisiana from suffering the same fate. In 1762, he gave it to his fellow Catholic majesty Charles III of Spain. As it turned out, that gift may have been unnecessary. English terms did not include transfer of New Orleans or Louisiana, west of the Mississippi.

America as a melting pot was never more apparent than in the names of characters serving Spain in the years that followed. St. Louis was founded during Spanish rule by French fur traders, including Auguste Chouteau, whose son and grandsons would play an outsized role in the expansion of steamboating into and through the Dakota Territory. Two surprising names in significant positions for the Spanish monarch were James Mackay and John Thomas Evans.

Mackay came to the northern plains as a fur trader, first by way of Canada and then continuing south to St. Louis, where he became the leader of a Spanish attempt best seen as their Lewis and Clark expedition. Evans was a Welshman in search of Welsh Indians. He landed in New York, made his way to St. Louis and found employment with Mackay.

With Evans as his lieutenant, beginning in August 1795, Mackay led a force of thirty-four men up the Missouri to a village of the Omaha, an earthlodge-dwelling people who had been trading with St. Louis merchants from the time the city was founded three decades previously. Mackay established a post he named Fort Charles, conducted some trade and determined to entrust Evans with the completion of the exploration. Mackay gave Evans very sensible orders about how to travel unobtrusively and warily to the Pacific Northwest. He was to avoid conflict with the Indians, whose territory he would be traveling through, and also with the Russians should he reach their outposts.

Mackay need not have bothered. Evans had his own agenda.

Evans canoed past the Arikara and Sioux and entered the Mandan-Hidatsa neighborhood on September 23, 1796. He commandeered the temporarily vacant trading post of French Canadian Rene Jessaume, whose trade route led back to Montreal. Evans raised a Spanish flag, unsuccessfully tried to communicate in Welsh with the natives and sent a message north declaring Spanish supremacy over the region and ordering the Canadian-based companies to stop trading with Spanish subjects. Writing for the Northwest Company, Cuthbert Grant, a leader of the Metís people of the Manitoba and Saskatchewan plains, who were just beginning to recognize themselves as a new nation, acknowledged King Charles's sovereignty over the Missouri River trade. He asked only that Northwest Company goods in the villages be withdrawn, as "indeed it has been my wish for some time past as we have lost a good deal of money by Mr. Gousseaume [Jessaume] whom we have employed in that business."[4]

Jessaume returned in March, bringing presents for prominent Mandan and Hidatsa. He tried to enlist them in a murder plot against Evans and, failing in that, took matters into his own hands and tried to shoot Evans. He was prevented by Evans's Indian translator, but after five months of no new trade goods coming from either the north or south, the Mandan and

Hidatsa had reasserted their rights to trade freely in February, when good-laden sleds came down from Canada. The Indians welcomed them with great ceremony and then expelled Evans from the villages in April, and their relationship with the Northwest Company continued as before.

Chapter 3

WELCOME TO THE UNITED STATES

The Norwester's were still there when Captains Lewis and Clark and the Northwest Corps of Discovery ascended the Missouri in 1804. Theirs was the first keelboat to reach deep into the Dakotas. It was a struggle. The *Discovery* was fifty-five feet long and eight feet wide with a three-foot draft. It had a mast that rose thirty-two feet. When wind allowed, a sail could be employed, but most of the progress against the five-mile-per-hour Missouri River current came by poling, or oars, or by men on shore or in the shallows step by step towing the boat by attached cordelles. It was hard work. In a later era, farther upriver, Lieutenant Saxton noted the ability of French boatmen "to endure an immense amount of fatigue and exposure" and to "toil on uncomplaining." He wished for the day when steamboats would supplant "this uncouth and laborious mode of navigating this magnificent river."[5]

The *Discovery* nosed past the mouth of the Big Sioux and into Dakota on August 21. The next day, the corps held an election to replace recently deceased Sergeant Charles X. Floyd. Patrick Gass won the first recorded election in the history of Dakota. The keelboat transected South Dakota in fifty-four days. Early on, with trader Pierre Dorian assisting, they met happily with the Yankton Indians and their old chief Arcawechar, who warned them that upriver Sioux would likely be less cordial. Dorian knew that was true from firsthand experience. As a trader at Régis Loisel's fort on Cedar Island, Dorian had been incessantly personally humiliated by the Partisan, a Brulé with a group of young men who openly expropriated trade goods. Lewis and Clark met the Brulé on September 23, and things didn't go well. Without Dorian, who remained with the Yankton for the winter, communication with the Brulé was difficult and tempers flared when the Americans failed to produce some gifts to secure passage through Brulé territory. It was the tensest moment of the entire expedition, with guns primed and aimed and hostile conversation. Brulé chief Black Buffalo, in the end, showed the restraint and reason that his colleague the Partisan and both captains did not, and the keelboat moved on to the Arikara villages at the mouth of the Grand River.

The Grand drains a substantial area of the border region between North and South Dakota to the west of the Missouri. The Arikara villages were on a very large island covered with earthlodge homes and gardens. On October 8, Lewis and Clark landed on the east side of the river and set up camp, and Lewis took a small party across to the island in a pirogue. Resident trader Joseph Gravelines's language skills and insights helped Lewis successfully convey the wishes of the United States for peace with and among the earthlodge nations. After nearly a week of conversation and rest, the expedition set out for the Mandan and crossed into what is now North Dakota on October 14. They met a Mandan hunting party on an island in the river on October 24 and reached the Mandan village of *Sheheke-shote*, White Coyote, on October 27, 1804. That's as far as the *Discovery* would go. The keelboat wintered at Fort Mandan and then returned with the April thaw downstream, picking up Indian chiefs to visit Washington.

The corps apparently intended to pull the boat and a pair of pirogues up onto the bank of the river, but a rapid two-foot drop in water levels lulled them into inaction as the boats found themselves beached on dry land. When the water rose again, the boats were trapped in ice. To preserve the *Discovery*, the men found themselves breaking up the ice around the boat in late January, a process that continued for a month, until they finally broke it free and, with windlass, timber and rope, drew it up on shore on February 26. On the first of April, it was returned to the water and on April 7 started downriver.[6]

Charles McKenzie of the Montreal-based Northwest Company lived with the Hidatsa from 1803 to 1805. His journals are well written and illuminating. They provide ethnographic information on the lives of his hosts, who were his friends. And as a friend, his narrative gives an insider's view of how Lewis and Clark's visit went over with the Hidatsa. It is particularly clear from McKenzie's report and later happenings that there was a big difference between the attitudes of the Mandan and the Hidatsa to the Americans. The Hidatsa and their leader Le Borgne leaned north to the Canadians. The Mandan, led by Sheheke-Shote, were more than eager to establish a relationship with the United States. Sheheke, in fact, agreed to accompany Lewis back to the nation's new capital to meet President Thomas Jefferson.

Even as the Corps of Discovery was heading back downriver with Sheheke, Rene Jessaume and their families in 1806, traders were coming up from St. Louis, hoping to establish relations for fur trade in the upper Missouri. In 1807, Manuel Lisa preceded a second group of traders traveling under military escort. Both were detained at the Arikara villages at the mouth of the Grand River near the current border between the two Dakotas.

The Arikara were angry that season. In the spring of 1805, while the Lewis and Clark expedition finished carving pirogues to proceed on their way to the Pacific, the keelboat that brought them to Fort Mandan returned to St. Louis. Along the way, *Discovery* gathered up chiefs to travel with them to the District of Columbia to meet President Jefferson. The Arikara chief *Arketarnawhar Was-to-ne*, Is-a-Whippoorwill, was one of seven chiefs to accept the invitation. Some difficulties delayed their trip from St. Louis to Washington, but it finally took place in 1806. Six of the seven guests, including Is-a-Whippoorwill, died while in the East. Veteran fur trader Joseph Gravelines got the unhappy assignment of delivering the chief's personal effects, \$200 or \$300 worth of gifts and a letter from Jefferson explaining the situation to the Arikara. He completed his assignment in the summer of 1807. The news was not well received. Gravelines, although a friend well known to the Arikara, was roughed up.

When Lisa arrived in August, he found the villages still riled. The Arikara demanded that Lisa forget about trading with the tribes to the north and release his goods to them. Lisa distributed some gifts and talked his way out of trouble. According to Nathaniel Pryor, Lisa's talk put Pryor into it. Lisa denied it.

The second trading group that season was a two-boat expedition led by Pierre Chouteau Sr. and escorted by Ensign Pryor and a group of forty-eight soldiers there to see Sheheke returned safely from his visit to the Presidential Mansion, which was yet-to-be named the White House.

At the lower of the two Arikara villages at the mouth of the Grand River, the Americans met a group of armed warriors on the beach. A Mandan female captive of the Arikara made her way to Pryor to deliver a warning. She told him Lisa had sold them out and the Arikara believed that all the goods on the two boats were meant for them. The Arikara also planned to kill Sheheke, she said, which comported with information Pryor had just received from a group of Sioux about a recent fight where Mandan had killed two Arikara at the Cannonball River. Pryor noticed that the Ree warriors were "checking their bullets and driving away their women and children." Despite his misgivings, Pryor went looking for someone he believed was a friend, chief Grey Eyes. He found him and arranged a council with him and other leaders to which Pryor delivered a standard speech of peaceful intent that included giving Grey Eyes a gift from William Clark. It was a peace medal. Pryor put it around the neck of Grey Eyes. It wouldn't stay there long.

While a couple of translators walked the shore, the boats proceeded to the second village where they found 650 warriors on the bank in a "violent rage." Pryor landed, but there were no councils or speeches here. An Arikara grabbed the cable of Chouteau's boat and waved to Pryor, dismissing him and the Mandan chief. Chouteau preferred not to be left behind. All pretense gone, the Arikara demanded all of Chouteau's guns and ammunition. Grey Eyes, rather than calming his warriors, ripped the peace medal from his neck and threw it to the ground. A warrior clubbed one of Chouteau's men to the ground, and the fight was on. Gunfire erupted, the Indians firing as they sought cover, the traders and soldiers cutting into them with a volley of swivel cannons, blunderbusses and small arms fire. A Hunkpapa named *Oglesa*, Red Shirt, was killed. Sioux visiting the village joined the Arikara in the fight.

Once the warriors reached cover, the battle settled into fixed combat at thirty to sixty yards. The advantages lay with the Indians. Their numerical superiority and protected firing positions made the superior armaments of the men on the beach irrelevant. Pryor determined to retreat with the current, and the boats cast off. Chouteau's got hung up on a sandbar, exposing crew to enemy fire as they worked to escape. A running battle of the floating boats versus warriors on both sides of the river lasted more than an hour, breaking off only at sunset.

In his report on the incident, Pryor concluded that fighting through the Arikara would require at least four hundred men and that one thousand might not be enough.[7]

There weren't a thousand men available in the West for President Jefferson to commit to such a mission. But he still insisted that his territorial governor, Meriwether Lewis, suggest a solution to safely return Sheheke to the Mandan. Lewis arrived at one in 1809. He hired a fur trade militia.

Pierre Chouteau Sr. was named its leader in the rank of major. Lewis organized the Missouri Fur Company with many of the prominent citizens of St. Louis, including two Chouteaus, William Clark, Meriwether's brother Reuben Lewis, Manuel Lisa and Andrew Henry, among others. The company received a no-bid contract with a fee of $7,000 to return Sheheke safely home on a covered barge. Chouteau was instructed to hire and arm 125 men, 40 of whom were to be expert American riflemen. Recalling Pryor's estimate of the force needed, Governor Lewis suggested that Major Chouteau recruit any trappers found along the way and that he should attempt to hire Sioux to join him in assaulting the Arikara village. He extended the contract with two payments totaling $940. The Missouri Fur Company would use the funds for gifts to the Sioux allies, who would be promised the plunder of the Arikara.

In *The Character of Meriwether Lewis*, Clay Jenkinson identifies denial of the $940 expense by the secretary of war as critical to Lewis's suicide a few months later. After being celebrated from St. Louis to Washington, the leader of the Corps of Discovery was named governor of the Louisiana Territory by his friend Thomas Jefferson. Jefferson's letters to Lewis after the Pryor fight showed a president losing his patience and a governor who didn't want to respond. When he finally committed to a course, the $7,000 contract with the Missouri Fur Company was approved by Jefferson's secretary of war, Henry Dearborn. But on March 4, 1809, James Madison was sworn in, and his secretary of war, William Eustis, saw no reason to increase the contracted amount and certainly not without preapproval. Lewis had to feel resentful. His judgment was questioned, his authority overruled and his personal wealth damaged, as he had to pay the $940 himself. But more, Lewis's deranged state of mind comes through most clearly in what he thought he was buying with that money.

Lewis recommended that Chouteau send spies ahead, men friendly to both the Americans and the Arikara. They were to gauge the level of hostile feelings at the villages and report back. If the Arikara seemed amenable to peace, they could have it on Lewis's terms, which seem hopelessly out of touch with reality. Peace could be had, if the Arikara identified the four warriors who had inflicted fatal wounds on Pryor's party. If they couldn't be identified, any four men would do. They were to be executed by firing squad in full view of the villagers. Not satisfied with blood, the governor would also require plunder. The Arikara would give a suitable portion of their horse herd to the Sioux.

Realizing that the Arikara might reject those terms, he recommended a surprise attack. It was Lewis's preferred alternative. The Arikara had to be punished, even "extirpated," for insulting the honor of the United States.

Fur traders don't want to exterminate Indians. They want to trade with them. Chouteau certainly scared the Arikara by drawing up in military fashion with cannon trained on the village, but the situation was never close to trouble. The river was open again. Manuel Lisa and Andrew Henry tried to extract some profit from it.

Lisa's 1807 trip past the Arikara had worked out quite nicely. At the Knife River villages of the Mandan and Hidatsa, Lisa walked from village to village handing out presents while his keelboat passed them. He went to the Yellowstone and then up it to the mouth of the Bighorn River where he wintered in Crow country. The Crow were friendly. They traded with him, and tolerated his men doing their own trapping. In 1808, he returned to St. Louis and cashed in profitable beaver pelts.

Other leaders in the community joined him in capitalizing expansion of the business. In 1809, Lisa was part of the Missouri Fur Company fleet of keelboats and barges going upriver from St. Louis with Sheheke and 350 men.[8] They took over the abandoned post of Régis Loisel on Cedar Island upstream from the mouth of the James and convenient to the Yankton and Brulé. The company built and staffed posts at the Knife River, the second Fort Mandan for trade with the Mandan and Hidatsa and their visitors, and at the Big Horn River, far up the Yellowstone, the company constructed Fort Raymond. From Fort Raymond, Andrew Henry set out with John Colter to the Three Forks area of the upper Missouri, which was Blackfeet country. They established Fort Henry there and a second Fort Henry across the Continental Divide. Both were abandoned within months because of constant hostility from the Blackfeet defending their own trap lines.

Colter's experience with the Blackfeet became a western legend. Colter and John Potts, both veterans of the Corps of Discovery, were checking their traps by canoe on the Jefferson fork when five hundred Blackfeet appeared on both sides of the creek and motioned the trappers to land. Colter directed the canoe to shore and disembarked. Potts panicked and backed the canoe into the stream. He was shot by an arrow. He fired a gun. So many arrows flew that Potts, in Colter's words, "was made a riddle of."

Rather than being killed out of hand, Colter was stripped and asked if he was a good runner. He said he was not, though trappers might think him swift. The unidentified chief of the band led a naked Colter to the prairie some three hundred yards in advance of the massed warriors. A war whoop sounded, and the race was on. Colter, barefoot on prickly pear, had motivation. He outran all but one warrior, who was so exhausted on catching Colter that his spear was thrown harmlessly. Colter picked it up, dispatched his enemy and continued his escape. He reached a river, dove in and, hiding under driftwood against an island, waited for nightfall. He swam silently downstream, and when feeling safer, he emerged to walk more than 225 miles to Fort Raymond, subsisting on a native staple—prairie turnips.

Despite trouble with the Blackfeet at the Three Forks, Lisa's business continued to invest in trade. He focused efforts lower on the Missouri and up the Yellowstone. He built another post for trade with the Hunkpapa, Cheyenne and Arikara at an oxbow in the Missouri near the North Dakota line. He allowed that to be named Fort Manuel. It was built under shadow of war. The United States was caught up in another war between England and France.

After the Congress of the United States declared war on England, on June 12, 1812, fur prices tumbled. Without access to the London or Leipzig markets, pelt prices dropped to $2.50 per pound from the $4.00 to $6.00 paid previously. Not only were profits sinking, but the smaller take was also harder to get. England sent runners to its old Indian trading partners south of Lake Superior and in Dakota and urged them to expel the Americans.

The Santee Sioux were encouraged, but Manuel Lisa undermined British efforts through his own contacts among the Indians. Remembering the war ten years after its beginning, the *St. Louis Enquirer* wrote about Lisa's successful efforts: "Every time they (Santees) started out to go to the lakes and Canada, runners would come and tell them that the Teton were coming to destroy their families and they were compelled to return to their homes to protect their women and children."[9]

During the War of 1812, Lisa "was a very smart man and he managed things so that all of the money and work of (Robert) Dickson to get the Santees to fight the Americans was lost. He got one of our men, (Tamaha, the one-eyed Sioux) to spy on his own people and let him know all that was being done. Father (Joseph Renville) met Lisa several times after the war, and he boasted about the way he managed the Tetons."[10] William Clark said during the war that Lisa "has been of great service in preventing British influence the last year." Lisa's biographer Walter P. Douglas concludes, "The settlers in Wisconsin, Michigan and the neighboring country who had never heard of Lisa were indebted to him for the preservation of their lives and property."[11]

Lisa was less successful in Dakota.

The Hidatsa and Crow were receptive to Dickson's message. Warriors from both nations killed and robbed trappers in 1812. When Lisa heard that two American hunters had been robbed of horses and killed by Hidatsa, he marched up from Fort Manuel to Big Hidatsa village for a confrontation. Hidatsa strongman Le Borgne received Lisa, acknowledged the theft and murders and refused to return the horses.

Le Borgne urged the Hidatsa to expel the Americans from their territory. Mandan leader Sheheke, on the other hand, considered himself "the brother of the president" of the United States.[12] In late September, Sheheke, two other prominent Mandan and eleven Hidatsa were killed in the only recorded battle between two nations who have grown hyphenated.[13]

Word of that battle came to Fort Manuel and clerk John Luttig on October 3. Ten weeks later, Luttig recorded the death by "putrid fever," considered possibly typhus or diphtheria, of Sacagawea, who had provided incalculable aid to the Lewis and Clark expedition. Fort Manuel was a nervous place that fall and winter. Rumors abounded, and guards were so on edge that one shot a dog he thought might be a skulking enemy.[14] The fort was abandoned in 1813.

The postwar period from 1815 to 1822 did not see rapid recovery of travel on the Missouri. The government of the United States was interested in the Missouri for security purposes, but fur prices didn't regain their prewar levels until about 1820, providing reason for little private investment.

Chapter 4

STEAM

At the Library of Alexandria around the start of the current era, a brilliant mathematician and teacher was also a tinkerer. Hero or Heron of Alexandria was, sans the immortal art, the Da Vinci of his age, a millennia and a half before Leonardo. He invented with both his mind and his hands, creating the world's first wind-powered machine, an organ and one of the world's first steam-powered machines, the *aeolipile.* By heating water to a boil in one chamber, Hero vented the expanding gas into a second, smaller chamber. The smaller chamber was a sphere mounted on a pivot with two small bent spigots, set on opposite sides of the sphere. As the steam escaped the sphere, it acted like a jet or a rocket force, causing the sphere to spin. It was a neat little toy. It had no practical application in the first century.

Hero apparently used the library to draw on earlier work by Ctesibius (285–222 BC), a Greek inventor and mathematician in Alexandria. Ctesibius wrote the first treatises on the science of compressed air and its uses in pumps. A near contemporary of Hero, Roman architect and military engineer Marcus Vitruvius Pollio, actually named the aeolipile and described them: "Hollow brazen vessels, which have an opening or mouth of small size, by means of which they can be filled with water. Prior to the water being heated over the fire, but little wind is emitted. As soon, however, as the water begins to boil, a violent wind issues forth."[15]

Hero took that and added a practical application. Steam, sent into the spherical second chamber, produced work. His instructions were:

> *Place a cauldron over a fire: a ball shall revolve on a pivot. A fire is lighted under a cauldron containing water, and covered at the mouth by the lid; with this the bent tube communicates, the extremity of the tube being fitted into a hollow ball. Opposite to the extremity place a pivot resting on the lid; and let the ball contain two bent pipes, communicating with it at the opposite extremities of a diameter, and bent in opposite directions, the bends being at right angles and across the lines. As the cauldron gets hot it will be found that the steam, entering the ball...passes out through the bent tubes towards the lid, and causes the ball to revolve, as in the case of the dancing figures.*[16]

As early as 1606, primitive steam methods were harnessed to replace horses in bringing water out of mines in Spain and Wales. The process evolved into the notoriously inefficient Newcomen engine. James Watt tinkered with repairing one in 1765 and hit on ways to improve it. Watt was not only an inventor but also a marketer. He measured the power of steam by how many horses it replaced, a measurement of work that continues today in auto and other engines as horsepower. Watt's name, of course, is also a measurement of power.

Watt took out a patent for a steam engine that reduced heat waste through the use of a condenser in 1769. It became a commercial success about a decade later, and the possibilities of steam power became realities.

John Fitch filed the first patent on a steamboat in America, which was granted in 1791. Fitch was already running a steamboat business for several years before the patent was approved due to a dispute with another inventor over who was first. Fitch demonstrated a steam-powered forty-five-foot-long boat to the delegates to the Constitutional Convention on the Delaware River in 1787. He operated a larger paddlewheel steamer for a few years carrying passengers and freight on a regular schedule between Philadelphia and Burlington, New Jersey. After a financial reversal, Fitch took his idea to France in 1793, hoping for, but not receiving, support from the revolutionary government.

A powerful member of the New York gentry, Robert Livingston was a man of many interests and great accomplishment. One of those interests was in steamboats, though they hardly existed when he was granted a hypothetical or, as it turned out, prospective monopoly on the steamboat business in New York State. He was also heavily involved in the shaping of the United States. Thomas Jefferson sent Livingston to France as ambassador in 1801, and by 1803, he was helping negotiate the Louisiana Purchase. While in Paris, he met Robert Fulton, who was there to convince the French to use his submarine design to blow up British shipping. That didn't work out, but Fulton and Livingston did demonstrate a steamboat on the Seine in 1802 and formed a partnership to do the same on the Hudson.

Long and skinny at 150 feet by 12 feet and known to history as the *Clermont*, for the Livingston family hometown, the *North River Steamboat* officially went into action on the Hudson in 1807. It ran a regular schedule from Albany to New York. Then Livingston and Fulton put a boat into operation in the West. Manufactured in Pittsburgh, *New Orleans* steamed down to work the lower Mississippi in 1811. It would be eight more years before a steamboat would nose into the Missouri.

Early engines were low pressure, featuring walking beams, a single vertical cylinder designed to produce maximum piston thrust on the vacuum stroke, though by the late 1810s or early '20s, high-pressure engines with horizontal cylinders and pitman arms driving counterweighted paddlewheels began to be used. Paired side-wheel engines were introduced in the mid-1820s, and the engine, firebox and boilers were moved to the main deck rather than being in the hold. Perhaps the best single book on the technological as well as the economic history of steamboating on the western rivers is Louis C. Hunter's classic *Steamboats on the Western Rivers*.[17]

Chapter 5

TESTING THE WATERS

As James Monroe was promoted from being simultaneously secretary of war and secretary of state to president, he began implementing a plan to secure the north-central border from British influences. A fort near St. Anthony Falls on the Mississippi and one parallel in latitude but hundreds of miles to the west on the Missouri would counteract a British post on the Red River at Pembina.

As a general plan became refined, the influence of Stephen H. Long began to be felt. Long was an engineer and an inventor and a major in the Corps of Engineers. He was sure that the vast distances of the West could best be secured to the United States by steamboats, which had first come west as a commercial enterprise in 1811, when Robert Fulton established service between Natchez and New Orleans on the lower Mississippi. In 1818, Secretary of War John C. Calhoun agreed with Long's vision and authorized the purchase of a steamboat for an expedition to establish a fort at the Mandan villages. In the national imagination, it became known as the Yellowstone Expedition, though the Yellowstone remained a long-range intention, not an immediate plan.[18]

Long suggested a small boat with a draft of no more than eighteen inches. Calhoun wanted to pay no more than $5,000 for it. No such boat existed. Undeterred, they determined to have one built. Long personally supervised construction of the *Western Engineer* in Pittsburgh over the winter of 1818–19. The boat was seventy-five feet long by thirteen feet wide. Loaded, it would draw two and a half feet. Unusual for the time, it was a stern-wheeler, Long anticipating what would become standard on the upper Missouri decades later. As a feature Long and colleagues thought likely to impress Indians, the *Western Engineer* looked like a boat riding a sea serpent with smoke from the boiler coming out of its mouth. Inevitably, it was called "Long's Dragon."

A test drive and subsequent redesign had the boat leaving Pittsburgh later in the year than planned. More delays came from additional mechanical problems as the boat came down the Ohio River. They didn't enter the Missouri until June 22, 1819. At Fort Bellefontaine, Long met the other two elements in the expedition, a force of soldiers under Colonel Henry Atkinson and their supply boats, a fleet of steamboats owned by the politically connected Johnson brothers, both veterans of the War of 1812. Richard Mentor Johnson of Kentucky was chairman of the Military Appropriations Committee of the U.S. House of Representatives. Recommended by movers and shakers, including 1812 War Hawks, Speaker of the House Henry Clay and Secretary Calhoun, his brother James received a no-bid contract to move and supply Atkinson's force. Not only wasn't it bid, the contract had no terms of compensation other than it would be "reasonable…equitable and just." The contract specified that Johnson would use steamboats, as they would have an impressive effect on the Indian nations. The *Western Engineer* would travel with Atkinson, but as a scientific expedition, it was not under his command.

"No operation extends with any certainty beyond the first encounter with the main body of the enemy," the Prussian field marshal Helmuth Von Moltke observed, in a phrase remembered more succinctly as no plan survives first contact with the enemy. In the case of the Yellowstone Expedition, the plans didn't survive to the start of the expedition. Johnson put five steamboats into operation to meet the *Western Engineer*, but only three made it to the Bellefontaine rendezvous point. They couldn't stay, as the sheriff was ordered to seize Johnson's boats to satisfy a $50,000 debt he owed to the Bank of St. Louis. Johnson had them steam out of the county, forcing Atkinson's men and supplies to follow to get on board. Though he fought back through his political connections, Johnson had a real problem. One boat, *Expedition*, made five miles a day between St. Louis and Fort Bellefontaine. The quartermaster general noted it drew seven feet and had "feeble" machinery. He was certain that it would not accomplish its goals. The *St. Louis Enquirer* wrote that Johnson's *Thomas Jefferson* "draws seven feet water when empty, five when loaded—is hog backed—and spends much of her time aground in a river half a mile wide and thirty feet deep." *Johnson*'s reviews were no better. A clerk on board said that it "was aground every day and frequently, at nights, we could look back and see the place we started from in the morning." He declared the whole fleet "totally unfit for the trip as could be."

The *Western Engineer* went ahead on June 21 while Atkinson wrestled with Johnson's steamboats and his own logistics. Two weeks later, the *Expedition*, *Thomas Jefferson* and *Johnson* followed, carrying Atkinson's troops. They labored for three days to cover the twenty-five miles to St. Charles. Atkinson was disappointed. He took his soldiers off the boats and walked to Fort Osage. The boats struggled along behind at a rate slower than keelboats moved. None of the Johnson boats made it to Council Bluffs. The *Jefferson* made less than two miles a day for two weeks before it snagged. The *Johnson* had many problems prior to its cylinder head exploding just above Fort Osage. The *Expedition* made it to Cow Island, where Martin Cantonment, the first U.S. military post in what became Kansas, greeted it and provided a place to winter.[19]

The terrible performance of the Johnson boats did not encourage continued experimentation with steamboats on the Missouri. It did expose an excellent example of crony capitalism or mercantilism in the early Republic. When the Johnson boats failed, the army had to contract with other rivermen to carry supplies in keelboats. Despite his failure, Johnson had already been paid $230,000 on his no-bid contract. Then he billed the government for another quarter million. Congress investigated and found that he'd either falsified or failed to provide documentation for over $60,000 in claims, but they paid up anyway. In fact, the investigation recommended that Johnson be paid nearly $20,000 more than he'd claimed.

The *Western Engineer* went back downriver in 1820 without reaching Dakota. Stephen Long's Yellowstone Expedition turned into a pedestrian affair. It would be another eleven years before a steamboat entered Dakota.

Chapter 6

THE ARIKARA WAR

Since the abolition of the United States factories, a great activity has prevailed in the operation of this trade. Those formerly engaged in it have increased their capital and extended their enterprises; new firms have engaged in it, and others are preparing to do so. It is computed that a thousand men, chiefly from this place, are now employed in this trade on the waters of the Missouri, and half that number on the upper Mississippi. The Missouri Fur Company, which alone employs upwards of 300 men, has reached the mountains and will soon be on the Columbia river. Others have the same destination, so that the rich furs of that region will soon cease to be the exclusive property of the Hudson Bay Company.[20]

Early in 1822, Missouri's elected lieutenant governor William Henry Ashley and his business partner, Andrew Henry, advertised in St. Louis for one hundred men to ascend the Missouri and enter the Yellowstone country, there to be employed for one, two or three years. His recruiting was successful. His recruits included Jed Smith and Hugh Glass, whose legend was misappropriated for *The Revenant*. The Ashley-Henry army—"Ashley's Hundred," as they came to be called—were deployed as trappers in contradiction of official United States policy. The policy was very much in dispute, as western interests considered it ridiculous to prevent Americans from conducting hunting and trapping in Indian country. Others understood the Indians' point of view and wanted to avoid trouble. Ashley's plans were criticized by the senior military leader on the frontier, Colonel Henry Leavenworth, as needlessly inciting Indian opposition. He knew his meager forces headquartered at

Fort Atkinson near Council Bluff would be unable to defend scores of trappers many hundreds of miles upriver.[21] The colonel was correct.

Andrew Henry led the first wave of recruits upriver in April, more concerned about getting a jump on the season than on being properly supplied, which would have delayed him only a few weeks. His expedition paid the price for his haste. With one keelboat and one hundred men between those on board and those marching along on shore, they set out on their adventure. The undersupplied group of inexperienced frontiersmen suffered privations, and many deserted. One unhappy employee said that even hunting game was impractical for the expedition. Several of his fellows were glad to get a dog to eat and even scavenged the skins of other cooked dogs to roast.[22] Despite desertions and a horse-stealing raid by Assiniboine, Henry's men reached the Yellowstone and established Fort Henry near the future site of fabled Fort Union. It was the third Fort Henry he had named after himself in his fur-trading career. None of them lasted long. This one was gone the next year, and a fourth Fort Henry was built up the Yellowstone at the mouth of the Big Horn River.

Meanwhile, his partner, Lieutenant Governor Ashley, worked on preparing the second wave. Fifty new employees departed St. Louis on May 8 on the keelboat *Enterprise*, carrying some $10,000 worth of supplies. The *Enterprise* hit a snag and sank three hundred miles upriver. The men were saved; the supplies were not.

Ashley was undeterred. He arranged additional credit and resupplied an expedition to meet his partner. His wife had passed away the previous November, and the legislature was not due to be in session until the next. Ashley would lead the second mission of 1822. Beginning with 46 men and a keelboat and picking up recruits along the way, as well as the survivors of the *Enterprise*, Ashley's party swelled to more than 125 men. With all the necessary stops at Fort Atkinson and Indian villages, including one of the Arikara's on September 8, he made remarkable time and reached Fort Henry in October.

The following year, Ashley's people and their keelboats, *Yellowstone Packet* and *Rocky Mountain*, were initially allowed passage, but in June 1823, while attempting to buy horses from the Arikara, a bad incident took place. Something went very wrong when a couple of Ashley's men slipped into the lower Arikara village looking for love in one of the wrong places. A fight in the village between individuals slipped out of the walls and became a war. Forty trappers under Jed Smith were camped on the beach in front of the palisades of the Arikara village. From about three thirty in the morning until dawn, the men on the beach and those on Ashley's two boats waited nervously while listening to war cries coming from behind the village walls. At dawn, the fight was on. Too late, Ashley had a plan to extricate the men on shore, but it couldn't be instituted in the mêlée of arrows and shot ripping through men and horses alike. Attempts to rescue the shore party by skiff added to the disaster. When the warriors flooded out of the village, the men on the beach fought for survival while attempting to swim to the boats, and like Pryor before, Ashley's Hundred retreated in their boats down the Missouri. Casualties were said by Ashley to be perhaps seven or eight Arikara and among his men twelve dead and eleven wounded. The war consisted of two battles—this fifteen-minute one and one in response.[23]

Colonel Henry Leavenworth brought troops and cannon from Fort Atkinson and, supplemented by Hunkpapa chief Five Hearts and other Teton Sioux bands, laid siege to the Arikara villages, shelling them into submission, and then allowing them to slip away in the night, much to the disgust of the Sioux and many in his own party. The Arikara temporarily moved north, belatedly accepting an offer of refuge previously offered by the Mandan. They built a town about a mile below the Mandan village of Mitutanka, reportedly on condition that they would cease making war on the Americans.

That didn't work. Too many Arikara were too angry. Five men out of St. Louis were killed by the Cannonball River and one trader at Tilton's Fort, adjacent to Mitutanka. The Mandan weren't happy, fearing that their new neighbors were inviting retribution. The Arikara weren't happy, being homesick for their abandoned villages. By the spring of 1824, they had returned to the Grand River to rebuild.[24]

Chapter 7

THE WHEEL BOAT PEACE ARMADA

Even before Lewis and Clark pulled, rowed and sailed their keelboat up the Missouri, patents had been applied for to outfit keelboats with working paddlewheels. Through a gear mechanism, the power of men or horses was used to turn twin paddlewheels, and the result was so appropriate to some situations that wheel boats, also known as horse boats or team boats, were used throughout the steam era and into the era of internal combustion. Horse-powered wheel boats were in use as ferries in St. Louis in 1819. General Henry Atkinson, while awaiting the steamboats assigned to the Yellowstone Expedition, saw those wheel boat ferries in action and "immediately conceived the idea of applying them to the barges bound up the Missouri with U. States troops, stores, etc. In about three days he had one of the barges rigged with wheels and a trial made in which she was run up the Missouri about two miles and back in 30 minutes."[25]

In 1823, Atkinson ran another trial of the wheel boat and concluded that they would be twice as fast going upriver as ordinary keelboats, and while they would be man-powered, the work of the men would be less hazardous to their uniforms than cordelling along the riverbank through mud and thickets. The last was part of a pitch to Secretary of War John C. Calhoun that the wheel boats would not be costly. Construction costs of the wheel machinery would be mitigated by not equipping the boats with masts and sails. In practice, General Atkinson was more or less wrong in each case. Wheel boat conversion cost more than Atkinson predicted, they did not forego having standard rigging of masts and sails, the soldiers' uniforms wore out as fast and the boats were not considerably faster than ordinary keelboats.

When the Arikara War had erupted, no steamboat had yet been beyond Fort Atkinson. None were used, and neither were wheel boats in Colonel Leavenworth's campaign of 1823. But for bringing a more regular military presence into Dakota, General Atkinson was sure that wheel boats were just the technological advancement he needed, and he got what he wanted.

In St. Louis in 1824, Atkinson took five keelboats out of service and converted them to wheel boats. A sixth wheel boat was constructed from scratch. It was christened the *Antelope* and was intended as the flagship of an armada to show the American flag to the several Indian nations of Dakota. The other boats were named for creatures that motivated the public-private partnership that was the fur trade: *Beaver*, *Mink*, *Otter*, *Muskrat* and *Raccoon*. The converted boats were sent up to Fort Atkinson in the late summer of 1824. The *Antelope* followed the next March, carrying a crew of twenty-three and a group of peace commissioners.

The *Antelope* didn't work well. Surprisingly, the converted boats did better. The *Antelope* would not accompany the expedition.

The 1825 wheel boat armada carried treaties, all standard in their provisions, with only a difference in introductory narrative about the current state of relations between the specific Indian nation and the United States. In the end, twelve were signed by at least ten leading members of the Indian group and ten non-Indian witnesses. After the U.S. Senate gave its consent, President John Quincy Adams signed them all on February 6, 1826. The treaties were one-sided. There were six provisions in each, except a seventh in the treaty with the Arikaras that served as a declaration that their recent war with the United States was concluded.[26]

1. *The sovereign Indian nations acknowledged by the signatures of their leaders that they were residents of the United States and that the United States had the right to regulate their trade.*
2. *"As may be convenient," the government of the United States would "from time to time" extend "benefits and acts of kindness."*
3. *The Indians were forbidden to trade with people from nations other than the United States.*
4. *The Indians would enforce that provision, protecting U.S. traders and capturing any foreigners in their region and turning them over to authorities of the United States.*
5. *Crimes by tribal members against whites would be prosecuted in U.S. courts. So would crimes by Americans against tribal members.*

6. *While intertribal trade was not forbidden, trade in guns or ammunition to Indian nations deemed hostile to the United States was not allowed.*

On May 16, 1825, an armada of eight boats left Fort Atkinson headed upriver. General Atkinson had gone all in on the wheel boat concept and added three more conversions christened the *Buffalo*, *Elk* and *White Bear*. Those three and the *Raccoon* were assigned to the Fourth Infantry, and the *Otter*, *Beaver* and *Muskrat* carried the Sixth Infantry. The flagship of the fleet was the *Mink*, carrying the General Atkinson, brigade staff and peace commissioners. The peace treaties would be made to seem more advantageous to the Indians by the 476 soldiers riding the wheel boats.

The wheel boats performed fairly well. There were mechanical kinks to work out on one boat or another, but the armada moved along well. Atkinson opined that they were faster than keelboats driven by even "select French crews"—that is, the best there was.[27]

Ten days after leaving Fort Atkinson, on May 26, the expedition passed Floyd's Bluff and entered the Dakotas. Floyd's Bluff is where the only member of the Lewis and Clark expedition to die is buried. Twenty-two years after his burial, both General Atkinson and Major Kearny noted the site as a landmark in their journals.

Dakota winds played hard with the boats' progress for a couple days as they approached the Vermillion River. Masts broke and were repaired, boats were driven to shore and travel delayed. The June rise came with the calendar and local rain. On June 1, General Atkinson noted that the river had risen two feet overnight. Kearny thought even more. Starting early the next day, they passed the mouth of the Vermillion and made good time to the mouth of the James River, passing it on June 4 and continuing past toward the site of modern Yankton. More equipment problems, not unique to wheel boats, and worse wind delayed them again, but finally, at midday on June 8, the armada reached its first objective for treaty making: the Ponca village on the Missouri at the mouth of White Paint Creek.

The Ponca were a small tribe of earthlodge dwellers, farmers and hunters who had been devastated by the smallpox epidemic that swept the western half of the continent in 1781. Recovering to about 450 individuals by 1825, the Ponca quickly accepted a treaty with the United States despite its one-sided nature. The treaty was signed on June 9, 1825, by He Who Makes Smoke, Child Chief, He Who Hides Something and other Ponca leaders.[28]

While the ceremonies proceeded, the boats were made ready, and so on the tenth, they were able to run against the current to the mouth of the Niobrara.

For the next week, they traveled steadily, slowed only by the facts that there were eight boats and one's trouble was everyone's. "Fresh sign of Buffalo & Elk coming to the river for water" and antelope and prairie dogs, chalk bluffs and berries, along with June weather in Dakota, entertained the expedition. Daily notes reveal no concern about its mission. On June 17, it reached Fort Kiowa, just above the mouth of the White River, across the Missouri from where Chamberlain is today. Built in 1822, the fur trade post had been involved with the Ashley-Henry efforts and had been the post to which Hugh Glass had crawled from the Lemmon, South Dakota area after being mauled by a bear and left for dead.

The Teton, Yankton and Yanktonnai were assembled together at Fort Kiowa by Indian subagent Peter Wilson. The Yankton and Yanktonnai were of the Nakota branch of the greater Sioux Nation. For five days, the expedition rested, conversed and exchanged gifts with the Sioux, who had begun to arrive on June 19, coincidentally accompanying another two-foot rise in the river.

The soldiers showed off a couple days later. The standard procedure for Atkinson's force was to order the brigade to assemble for review, fire off some guns and particularly try to impress the Indians with rockets and cannon fire. On June 22, the treaty was signed by Black Bear, Flying Medicine, Mad Buffalo, Hollow Bear and two dozen other men of the Yankton and Yanktonnai.[29] The armada moved on the following day. Atkinson believed that his next meeting would be one hundred miles northwest, around the Big Bend with the Saone and Oglalla bands of the Lakota at the mouth of a river he called Little Missouri, others called Teton and we now call Bad River, which enters the Missouri across the river from the state capital of Pierre, South Dakota.

They got there without incident and went into camp on June 30. They spent several very hot summer days angling the Bad River, impressed with the catfish. They took inventory, distributed six buffalo brought in by their hunters and had a general court-martial called by General Atkinson and immediately adjourned by the junior officers of the court as being improperly constituted.

One hundred lodges of Oglalla came near Camp Teton on July 2, causing orders to be issued restricting the number of men who could be absent from camp at one time, telling them to avoid the Indian camp and to go about armed and announcing that the firing of a cannon should bring everyone running. These sensible precautions proved unnecessary. On Independence Day, while soldiers temperately enjoyed an extra gill of whiskey, the Oglalla graciously hosted a conference, including Saone and Cheyenne leaders, in a lodge in the Oglalla village. They smoked, ate boiled dog and drank river water from buffalo bladders while seated on buffalo robes and beaver pelts. The peace commissioners were each given their respective hides.

A treaty signing was scheduled for the following day and papers prepared for the Oglalla and Saone, but the Saone asked for another day so late arrivals could participate. On July 6, treaties with all three tribes were signed. Chief among the signators were Siounes (Saone) leaders Rushing Man, Crow Feather, White Swan and Two Lance. For the Oglalla were Standing Buffalo, Shoulder, Full White Bear and Ghost Boy.[30] The expedition continued upriver the next day. On July 12, the treaty making caught up with the Fire Hearts Band of Sioux at Camp Hidden Creek. Chief Fire-Heart, along with One That Shoots as He Walks and One That Makes a Noise as He Flies added their names to the agreement dated July 5.

The final group of Lakota to sign the treaty were the Hunkpapa on July 16. Signators included Little White Bear, White Bear's Face, White Elk, One That Has No Name, Womb and Arikara.[31]

Two days later, Atkinson wrapped up the agreement with the Arikara, formally ending the state of war that had existed since 1823. Arikara chiefs signing were Bloody Hand, Little Bear, Skunk, Bad Bear, Fool Chief and Chief That Is Afraid.[32]

On July 30, at the lower Mandan village, signatures were obtained from both the Mandan and the Hidatsa, named *Belantse-etea* in the document. Mandan signators designated as chiefs were Little Crow, Wolf Chief, Chief of Four Men and Bear That Does Not Walk.[33] The Hidatsa had nine chiefs sign: Wolf Chief, One That Makes the Road, Crow That Looks, Guard of the Red Arrows, Dog Bear, Black Buffalo, Black Moccasins, One That Carries the Snake and Oh-Sha-Lah-Ska-A-Tee.[34] As the armada moved on, it left behind an unintended gift, a pair of Norwegian rats, one male and one female. Elizabeth Fenn explains that the rats were initially celebrated, as they were observed killing the mice that had tried to share the villagers' garden produce for centuries. Then the rats turned out to be the greater thieves.[35]

The final meeting was with the Crow on August 4. Sixteen men were noted as chiefs. The first signatures were from Long Hair, One That Sings Bad, One That Rains, Wolf's Paunch and Little Black Dog.[36] The wheel boats turned and ran with the current back to Fort Atkinson.

The trip was a moderate success. The wheel boat armada didn't lead to a new era in boats, but it definitely calmed the great highway that was the Missouri. Trading posts started springing up in our region, and Indian agents did extend some benefits to the tribes. By 1828, construction started at Fort Union, and faster travel up the Missouri was needed.

Chapter 8

GIVE IT STEAM

Boat travel from St. Louis to Fort Union was problematic from the start. Where the Mississippi is deep and wide, the Missouri is merely wide. Most of the year, it was either too frozen or too shallow for heavily laden keelboats. There were two generally reliable rises in the river. The first was at ice out and prairie snow melt in March or April. The second rise was in June, when the mountain snowmelt filled the Montana tributaries. At the speed of a keelboat, it took months to go from St. Louis to the Yellowstone; going downriver, of course, was faster and easier.

Steamboats came to Dakota Territory to make profit. Their presence had many other implications and consequences, but the motivation for building the first boats powered by steam engines to reach what became the Dakota Territory was quite unlike the idealistic pronouncement of Antoine de Saint Exupery: "When you want to build a ship, do not begin by gathering wood, cutting planks and distributing the work, but rather create in men a yearning for the vast and endless sea." In the case of the *Yellow Stone*, the ship was built in 1830 by practical professionals in Louisville for a fee, and it was commissioned by capitalists in New York who were willing to take a financial risk in exchange for pretty remarkable financial gains. The profit motive was there at the start, and it remained firmly ensconced in the Missouri River steamboat business for as long as it was conducted.

Steamboats had been used on the lower Missouri since 1819, and there were many successful boats on the Mississippi between St. Louis and New

Orleans and more on the Ohio River. Many robes and furs that left Dakota on keelboats or mackinaws were loaded on steamboats in St. Louis and steamed up the Ohio on their way to New York, avoiding the fur-damaging humidity of the Gulf Coast summer. The upper Missouri remained a precinct unvisited by steam, even as it sprouted trading posts in the 1820s.

KENNETH McKENZIE

Born: April 15, 1797, Rosshire (or Bradlack), Scotland
Died: April 26, 1861, St. Louis, Missouri

"The King of the Upper Missouri" was what people called him—and for good reason. Kenneth McKenzie emigrated from Scotland to Montreal in his nineteenth year, 1816. He spent six years learning the fur trade while working for the Northwest Company, the major competitor to the Hudson's Bay Company in the Canadian West. His future lay in the American West. McKenzie became one of the leading employees of the Columbia Fur Company.

Astor's American Fur Company absorbed McKenzie with the Columbia Fur Company in 1827. It established, in 1828, a very large trading center for the native people from the Rockies to the plains of Dakota. Eventually called Fort Union, its twenty-foot-high whitewashed cottonwood walls rising on the north bank of the Missouri River, just a mile upstream from its confluence with the Yellowstone River, were meant to be impressive, and they were. Kenneth McKenzie became the new fort's bourgeois. The Bourgeois House within the fort walls was a bit of American elegance alone on an otherwise rough frontier.

In order to make his new post profitable, McKenzie argued in favor of it being supplied by steamboat from St. Louis. The company, operating as the Upper Missouri Outfit (UMO) division of the AFC, agreed and ordered the *Yellow Stone* built. It was named aspirationally.

A decade of steamboat operation on the lower river had helped the evolution of boat construction. The *Yellow Stone* was a side-wheeler, the style most common around St. Louis at the time. It would appear primitive and inefficient compared to the shallow-draft, low-profile mountain boats of a later era, but it would suffice to make historic voyages in Dakota Territory and to be the boat that saved Texas, according to Sam Houston, someone who should know.

Delivered to St. Louis from Louisville on April 10, 1831, the *Yellow Stone* was quickly loaded for its penetration of the river above Council Bluffs, today Omaha, Nebraska. It carried a crew of twenty-two and another seventy-five passengers, including company officers and new workers for its series of upriver trading posts. The captain was Bernard Young. Upper Missouri Outfit head Pierre Chouteau Jr. went along for the ride. The boat was named for its destination, but it didn't reach it in 1831. It did reach Dakota and then bogged down.

Knowing the *Yellow Stone* was not exactly suited to the shallow Missouri, Chouteau had it leave St. Louis just six days after its arrival, hoping to take advantage of the spring rise. It worked past the Yankton area to the mouth of the Niobrara River in late May, where they found the boat was carrying too much weight to continue. A June rise was expected, but in the meantime, Chouteau sent runners to the UMO's Fort Tecumseh, two hundred miles upstream by modern-day Pierre. The fort's bourgeois dispatched two keelboats to relieve the *Yellow Stone*. Supplies were offloaded, and the *Yellow Stone* continued upriver. It reached Fort Techumseh on June 19. The June rise was insufficient to encourage further experiment, and the *Yellow Stone* returned to St. Louis in triumph, despite undershooting its destination. A profitable return of buffalo robes and other furs, along with five tons of buffalo tongues, was good news for the company, and the steamboat era was begun.

The following year, *Yellow Stone* reached its namesake river. Andrew Bennett captained, and Chouteau again accompanied. A paying passenger was artist and ethnologist George Catlin on a mission to chronicle Indian culture before it gave way to the expanding United States. Captain Bennett got a good jump on the navigation season, leaving St. Louis on March 26, allowing the boat to spend a few days at new Fort Pierre, a replacement for Fort Tecumseh, at the beginning of June. With the 1832 June rise, *Yellow Stone* had no trouble reaching Fort Union. It could have gone much farther, up either the Yellowstone or Missouri, but there was no commercial purpose. The boat deposited supplies and passengers and loaded furs and robes, a cargo profitably delivered to St. Louis.

After that, one boat or more ascended the river annually. The *Yellow Stone* took Prince Maximilian and Karl Bodmer up to Fort Pierre in 1833, where they transferred to a new boat, *Assiniboin*, which took them to Fort Union in 1833. *Yellow Stone* went on to make history in the Texicans' rebellion against the Mexico that had welcomed them but was now attempting to ban slavery. *Yellow Stone* served as a mobile capitol, hospital ship, troop ship and supply ship for the secessionists. It hosted the formal surrender of a wounded Santa Anna to Sam Houston. Houston said it was the boat that saved Texas.

Splitting time between Fort Union and Fort Clark, which was adjacent to the Mandan and Hidatsa villages near the mouth of the Knife River, George Catlin dove into his work. He had declared that his life was to be "devoted to the production of a literal and graphic delineation of the living manners, customs, and character of an interesting race of people, who are rapidly passing away from the face of the earth—lending a hand to a dying nation, who have no historians or biographers of their own." His paintings illustrate and freeze in time scenes of public life, games and ceremonies. They are joyful. His writings are perceptive and less judgmental than is usual in his era. He was a fan of the Mandan, particularly.

He had a one-year jump on two European visitors, one an artist superior to Catlin and the other a much more detailed anthropologist.

Chapter 9

FORT UNION'S VISITORS

When the steamboat *Assiniboin* steamed into sight of John Jacob Astor's Fort Union Trading Post's tall, whitewashed cottonwood walls, Prince Alexander Philipp Maximilian zu Wied-Neuwied waxed eloquent:

> *At the next turn of the river, towards the right hand, we had a fine prospect. Gentle eminences, with various rounded or flat tops, covered with bright verdure, formed the back-ground; before them, tall poplar groves, and willow thickets on the bank of the river, whose dark blue waters, splendidly illumined by the setting sun, flowed, with many windings, through the prairie. A little further on lay Fort Union, on a verdant plain, with the handsome American flag, gilded by the last rays of evening, floating in the azure sky, while a herd of horses grazing animated the peaceful scene.*[37]

The scene got more animated shortly, as hundreds of Assiniboine arrived and set up camp around the fort. Approaching in an order that reminded Maximilian of "two bodies of infantry," they had come to trade, not fight. For guns, ball and powder, metal tools and manufactured articles of clothing, the Assiniboine brought hides and furs: otter, weasel, marten, lynx, red fox, cross fox, silver fox, mink, muskrat, deer and, likely, elk and antelope. The biggest trading items were beaver and buffalo. Twenty-five thousand beaver pelts were taken in by the traders at Fort Union in 1832. They received nearly twice as many buffalo robes.

Fort Union Trading Post National Historic Site, May 2016, NPS/Fred MacVaugh. *Courtesy of Fort Union Trading Post NHS.*

The American Fur Company's trade in buffalo robes not only was profitable in and of itself but also signaled a serious competitive advantage over the Hudson's Bay Company. The weight and bulk of a buffalo robe, or fifty thousand of them, was an insurmountable problem for the canoe and sled trade necessary to get products from the Rockies to the forts reachable by the company's York boats. If the Assiniboine, Blackfeet, Gros Ventre, Piegan and other tribes of the border region couldn't trade robes to the British, they would trade robes and beaver plews to the Americans.

Assiniboin returned to St. Louis from Fort Union on July 11, 1833, carrying profit. In 1834, *Assiniboin* reached Fort Union on June 26 and then went another eighty miles upriver, setting a new upper Missouri penetration record for a steamboat. The record would stand for seventeen years. And there, trapped by low water, it was forced to remain for the winter. An armed guard encamped alongside.

In April, the crew freed the boat from ice and set out to return with its profitable cargo to St. Louis, but across from the mouth of the Heart River, at Sibley Island, south of the future site of Bismarck, *Assinboin* caught fire and burned. The fire started in a passenger cabin and quickly spread. The boat and cargo were uninsured. The survivors were the crew, passengers and five live buffalo the humans found time to release to their own recognizance as the flames consumed the boat. Losses were estimated at perhaps $80,000, more than $2 million in 2016 currency. More importantly to Prince Maximilian, the losses included specimens for his naturalistic studies.

Prince Maximilian traveled with an artist on retainer, Karl Bodmer. The Swiss-born Bodmer was just twenty-three when the veteran German explorer, then forty-nine, hired Bodmer to accompany his second journey to the Americas. If ethnology had been a recognized field of science at the time, Maximilian would have been a foremost authority, having studied under Alexander Von Humboldt and led his own exploration of the indigenous peoples of southeastern Brazil in his early thirties.

In 1832, the upper Missouri was a place of high adventure to a European mind. The Indian nations there were considered just beyond the degrading influence of European culture and existing in as close to a state of original grace as could be found outside the Amazon rainforest or parts of Africa. The truth was, naturally, quite different. The people of the region had been transformed and cultures changed greatly in the previous century. Horses and guns were not just commercial trade items; they were part of an arms race and key components in the movement of peoples responding to intertribal warfare. Whatever the reality, the perception remained, and the changed reality remained a compelling attraction for study. After the introduction of horses and guns, the Plains nations were developing a completely new culture and geopolitical order, and it was, as it remains, fascinating.

While Bodmer painted detailed, realistic portraits of various tribal members, Maximilian made friends. He asked questions. He made notes. Where Catlin was an obvious fan of the lifestyle of the Mandan, particularly, Maximilian's writings take a much more objective tone. His training, too, seems to come through in his questions probing standard ethnology. Where Catlin saw and drew the burial scaffolds and a shrine of skulls, it was Maximilian who asked his Mandan companions why they do not bury their dead in the ground. The answer he got explains a lot about why skeletons are found in Mandan cache pits. "The Lord of Life told us we came from the earth and should return to it. But not long ago we began to leave the dead aboveground, because we love them and want to cry at the sight."[38] Maximilian's three-volume set of *The North American Journals of Prince Maximilian of Wied* is the most essential guide to the Mandan and Hidatsa of any written between the devastating smallpox epidemics of 1781 and 1837.

Another renowned artist and observer came to Fort Union a decade later, largely to observe and paint the native flora and fauna, particularly the viviparous quadrupeds. John James Audubon arrived on the steamboat *Omega* in 1843. It had been a record-setting run in a high-water spring. Captain John Sire and his pilot, twenty-seven-year-old Joseph La Barge, arrived at Fort Union forty-nine days after leaving St. Louis.

Already a successful artist and famous naturalist, Audubon spent months as a guest at Fort Union. He killed and painted birds and observed the region's fur trade at its height. He may have appreciated the birds. He had little good to say about the fort's accommodations or its traders of any ethnicity.

Given that he was quite insulting toward native peoples in his writings, his respect for one Blood Indian woman was all the more remarkable. *Natoyist-Siksina'*, known to most of her contemporaries as Natawista or Mrs. Alexander Culbertson, was, to Audubon, a true "Indian Princess." It was a fair characterization, with emphasis on both words.

The princess part came from her dignified and commanding personality; her status as a favored daughter of Two Suns, a respected chief of the Fish Eaters Band of Bloods, and the sister of his respected successor; and being the wife of the chief trader of the Missouri Fur Company to the Blackfeet bands, including the Northern Blackfoot, Piegan and Blood Indians. The Indian part came from observation of her mastery of traditional native skills and her impressive physical abilities, including being a "most expert and graceful" swimmer and "a wonderful rider, possessed of both strength and grace in a marked degree."

Audubon saw her comfortable in her role as the eighteen-year-old female head of household in the Bourgeois House at Fort Union, elegantly presiding over dinners and balls, dressed in European-style finery. She was "handsome, and really courteous and refined in many ways." Then he saw Natawista and her maid dressed in the Indian-style racing across the prairie with her husband and two other men. "The Ladies had their hair loose, and flying in the breeze, and then all mounted on horses with Indian saddles and trappings. Mrs. Culbertson and her maid rode astride like men, and all rode a furious race, under whip the whole way, for more than one mile on the prairie." Audubon noted her "magnificent black hair floating like a banner behind her." The men, he thought, "ran like wild creatures of unearthly compound."

With Audubon watching, Natawista went mallard catching in the Missouri. With her expert and graceful swimming, she caught six live mallards while he watched. Audubon's words jump off the page, setting imagination loose on exactly how she accomplished that. He also saw her working on a parfleche, incorporating golden eagle feathers. She'd killed the eagle herself.

There is much more to say about Natawista, and Lesley Wischmann has said it in a really fine dual biography published by the Arthur H. Clark Company in 2000. The completely appropriate title is *Frontier Diplomats: The Life and Times of Alexander Culbertson and Natoyist-Siksina'*.

The 1840s were the only full decade of steamboat traffic in Dakota devoted exclusively to the fur trade. Traders like Culbertson and indigenous personalities like Natawista were essential go-betweens, uniting the producers of the interior with world markets. Tensions existed, to be sure, between company trappers, free traders and native bands, but military occupation of Dakota was still in the future.

Depletion of the resource and a changing fashion trend reduced the influence of beaver in the trade. In fact, in Fort Union's first decade, the fur trade began shifting to the robe trade, a change advantageous to men with steamboats on the Missouri and a welcome change for the Plains Indians, who were more inclined to hunt buffalo and use every part than they were to trap beaver. One part of the bison, the robe, became money.

In exchange for beaver, mink and other pelts and for hundreds of thousands of buffalo robes, St. Louis sent up goods from around the world. And that's where the hides and furs went—from St. Louis to New Orleans or New York and on to London, Leipzig and China.

By the time of the steamboat era, buffalo robes were the biggest trade item. Beaver for top hats was the most expensive per pound—$2.50 for much of the period. Buffalo robes, which weigh fifteen to twenty pounds or more, went for about that much a piece, not a pound.

Three robes would bring an Assiniboine one three-point wool blanket four feet by six. Two robes would get a two-gallon brass kettle. That hit the indigenous pottery industry hard. A single robe could get three butcher knives, one hundred loads of powder and shot or a yard of colored red or blue cloth.

It took ten robes to get a horse or a gun. All of this was subject to quality on both sides of the equation. Crow were reputed to bring in the best-dressed robes. American-made products were generally inferior to European and, in some cases, Chinese imports. American-made kettles, awls, tomahawks, bells, bangles, hoes, pipes and tobacco were fine, but the native people preferred British guns and blankets, French gunpowder, Venetian beads and Belgian and German guns. Vermillion was popular, too, Chinese more than American. Vermillion is a mercury-based red paint that must have caused untold harmful health consequences for the users.

Using buffalo hides as a form of currency suited the lifestyle of the Plains Indians. All other hides and furs were figured as so many beaver pelts or racoon hides equaling one robe. The introduction of a "price" schedule into the native economy meant something important. Whether the buffalo hunter thought about the one hundred loads of powder and shot he would get when he let fly an arrow is unknowable, and the robe itself always had both intrinsic and trade value; however, now it had a baseline value measured in a variety of products. Buffalo robes had become money.

Chapter 10

VOYAGE OF DEATH

The St. Peters

The steamboat *St. Peters* was the newest boat of the Chouteau, Pratte & Company in 1837. The loss of the *Assiniboin* and its cargo in 1835 had been devastating. John Jacob Astor retired from the fur trade in 1834 and sold assets to the people who had been operating them for him. As long as there was a fur business in the upper Missouri, there was a member of the St. Louis Chouteau family heavily involved with the dominant company. Pierre Chouteau ran the Upper Missouri Outfit for Astor's American Fur Company. Bernard Pratte had captained *Assiniboin* in 1833 for the company. When Astor looked to sell out, Chouteau and Pratte reformed the Upper Missouri Outfit as Chouteau, Pratte & Company. One of the assets they bought was *Assiniboin* while it was far up the Missouri on its last voyage. With no insurance and no return on the investment in *Assiniboin*, the company was born in trouble. *St. Peters* was intended to get them out of it.

St. Peters was a longer, but lighter boat than *Assiniboin*, another step in the evolution of boats intended for the upper Missouri. It was 139 feet long and 19 feet wide compared to 120 feet long and 20 feet wide for *Assiniboin* and weighed only 119 tons compared to 149 tons for the unfortunate steamboat. Both boats, and *Yellow Stone* before them, were side-wheelers. Built in 1836 in Pittsburgh, it was delivered to St. Louis and outfitted for its first trip to Fort Union.

On April 17, 1837, *St. Peters* departed St. Louis with Bernard Pratte in command. They reached Fort Leavenworth in twelve days. That's where the first sign of trouble appeared. One of the workers, identified only as a "Mulato," became ill, complaining of back pain. A steamboat worker complaining of back pain must not have been an uncommon thing. In any event, it didn't initially cause concern, at least not to the captain. Two days after the onset, it was suggested that the sick man be put off the boat. Pratte refused, contending that it was a stomach upset and prescribing ipecac.[39]

Before the boat reached Council Bluffs, doubt about the condition was removed. Smallpox was fully developed in the first patient, and other people had been infected.

It should be noted that vaccination against smallpox had advanced by the 1830s and no longer involved actually giving patients smallpox, which even with the best care could still cause death in one out of twenty or twenty-five patients. Cowpox provided a vaccine that was given, by act of Congress, to the potentially vulnerable tribes. As early as 1831, cowpox vaccine was protecting Indians along the Missouri. Indian agent John Sanford sent vaccine to Fort Tecumseh, an opposition trading post near Fort Pierre. Whether or not it was widely distributed among the local Lakota and Dakota is uncertain. In no case did it reach or surpass the Arikara villages. Secretary of War Lewis Cass had declared that "under no circumstance" would any effort be made to vaccinate Indians above the Arikara.

So, as the ever-more-appropriately-named *St. Peters* worked its way up the Missouri it found an ever-more receptive population for *Variola major*, one of mankind's most serious killers for thousands of years. Until the cowpox vaccine, the only immunity to smallpox was having survived it. The only Mandan, Hidatsa, Arikara, Crow or Assiniboine with immunity to smallpox were the elders who had survived the 1781 epidemic.

No citizens' brigade came out to quarantine or drive away the boat, as happened with cholera on *Yellow Stone* in Missouri in 1833. Ironically, it was Bernard Pratte as captain of the *Assiniboin* who had pointedly ignored pleas for help for *Yellow Stone*'s emergency captain, young Joseph La Barge, as *Assiniboin* passed down to St. Louis. Pratte apparently wanted nothing to do with a communicable disease. In the 1837 situation, *St. Peters*, knowingly carrying smallpox as of at least May 1, continued on its route. It even took on passengers.[40]

In the years after the wheel boat armada treaty with the Arikara in 1825, the earthlodge people had struggled against Lakota dominance. In 1832, they left the Grand River and went on an exodus. First, they tried farming in Nebraska alongside other Caddoan-speaking earthlodge dwellers. In 1835, they made the unusual shift from being farmers to being nomadic. That lasted less than two years. In the spring of 1837, the entire Arikara Nation, two thousand strong, decided to try again to be good neighbors to the Mandan.[41]

As goods were being unloaded and passengers fled the boat at Council Bluffs, three Arikara women with several children boarded *St. Peters* and asked for passage to join their nation by Mitutanka, at the mouth of the Knife River.

People started dying, though the original patient had recovered, both facts coming from Pratte's recollection. The Arikara became obviously ill with smallpox. The boat proceeded on, unloading goods and people at Fort Pierre. It also took on new passengers. Jacob Halsey was assigned to take over as the Bourgeois at Fort Union. His very pregnant wife and son boarded *St. Peters* with him. She delivered within three weeks, suffering from smallpox. She and her infant daughter died. Halsey had a "discreet" case and survived.[42]

Before *St. Peters* reached Fort Clark, its clerk Francis Chardon left his post to meet the boat downriver. He found it just south of the Square Buttes, rather near the ancient abandoned village of Yellow Clay, known today as Double Ditch state historic site. It is unclear if Chardon saw the extent of the danger the boat was carrying, but he climbed aboard and steamed to Fort Clark, where the boat was met with enthusiasm, "all hands a Frolicking."

In later years, Chardon would recall sending runners to the Mandan and Arikara out hunting to tell them to stay away from their villages and Fort Clark for some time. He didn't mention doing that in his journal, so that memory may have been inserted to absolve himself from responsibility for what happened next. Even if it were an accurate recollection, telling the hunters that there was illness among their loved ones back in their villages was not a deterrent to their returning.

Others, including Pratte, came up with similar excuses why it was not their negligence or desperation for profit that killed thousands of people. They had a story concocted to blame the victim. The spread of smallpox wasn't from the many people and goods that had come into contact with it. Instead, it was a thieving Arikara who had swum from shore in the night, snuck on *St. Peters* and stolen a blanket from a smallpox sufferer. Now, why anyone would go to such lengths in pursuit of an infected blanket was never discussed. The excuse got repeated for decades. It's unknowable whether anyone anywhere ever believed the ridiculous story.

Chardon's journal at Fort Clark notes how many rats were killed in the fort each month. After *St. Peters* visited, Chardon began reporting deaths of his trading partners. On July 14, not quite four weeks after the steamboat's arrival at Fort Clark, Chardon noted, "A young Mandan died to day of the Small Pox—several others has caught it." A fresh case came to his attention July 17, and news from the Arikara village was that smallpox had appeared. There were undoubtedly deaths that did not merit mention from Chardon, who frankly had nothing but disrespect for the Mandan, with the exception of one of their chiefs, Four Bears, *Mato Tope*. On July 26, he notes that smallpox broke out in the smaller Mandan village and that several had died. Four more died the next day.

On July 28, the Mandan and Arikara put on two splendid dances. They told Chardon that "as they expect to all die of the small pox—and as long as they are alive, they will take it out in dancing."

On the thirtieth, word came from the Hidatsa that ten or fifteen had died, including a couple of prominent leaders. Four Bears died, too. His recorded speech about his impending death is chilling.

> *My friends one and all, listen to what I have to say. Ever since I can remember, I have loved the Whites. I have lived with them ever since I was a boy, and to the best of my knowledge, I have never wronged a White man. On the contrary, I have always protected them from the insults of others, which they cannot deny. The Four Bears never saw a White man hungry, but what he gave him to eat, drink, and a buffalo skin to sleep on, in time of need. I was always ready to die for them, which they cannot deny. I have done every thing that a Red skin could do for them, and how have they repaid it! With ingratitude!*
>
> *I have never called a White man a dog, but today, I do pronounce them to be a set of black-hearted dogs. They have deceived me, them that I always considered as brothers, have turned out to be my worst enemies.*
>
> *I have been in many battles, and often wounded, but the wounds of my enemies I exalt in. But today I am wounded, and by whom, by those same White dogs that I have always considered, and treated as brothers. I do not fear death, my friends. You know it, but to die with my face rotten, that even the wolves will shrink with horror at seeing me, and say to themselves, that is the Four Bears, the friend of the Whites.*
>
> *Listen well what I have to say, as it will be the last time you will hear me. Think of your wives, children, brothers, sisters, friends, and in fact all that you hold dear, are all dead, or dying, with their faces all rotten, caused by those dogs the Whites. Think of all that my friends, and rise altogether and not leave one of them alive. The Four Bears will act his part.*[43]

On August 6, one Arikara died, according to Chardon. Over the next four days, he reported six or seven deaths. On August 10, that became twelve to fifteen; he wasn't certain. On August 11, Chardon gave up. "I Keep no a/c of the dead, as they die so fast that it is impossible."

Others among the Mandan, Hidatsa and Arikara had the same view as Four Bears, that the whites were responsible and should be killed. The steamboat was to blame, the Indians believed, and they were correct. Individuals came with cocked guns and murderous intent, but all violent acts were deflected. The three nations were too devastated to carry through the threats.

The five villages at the mouth of the Knife River emptied. More than 80 percent of the Mandan died, and the other earthlodge people were also devastated, though perhaps not as badly as they had been in 1781. Where there had been perhaps ten thousand Mandan in seven villages before 1781, there were about two hundred individuals left after 1837. The Arikara are estimated to have lost 30 percent of their population to the 1837 epidemic. Hidatsa mortality was about 50 percent.[44]

The Mandan and Hidatsa joined together into one village, Like-a-Fishhook, farther upriver. Fort Berthold was established nearby. The days of independent cities being over, there was some attempt to at least have separate neighborhoods in Like-a-Fishhook. The Arikara temporarily moved into the abandoned Mandan city, but eventually, pressured by the Hunkpapa and Yanktonnai, they joined the others at Fort Berthold. The three tribes continued to trade with, and became militarily dependent on, the United States.

Captain Pratte's voyage was a standard capitalistic nearsighted success without regard for long-term effects on people or even future profits that could have been generated by the people who were killed by the pursuit of short-term profit. *St. Peters* spread the smallpox at Fort Union as well, and perhaps continued to spread it as it slid downstream accompanied by mackinaws, all "laden with furs."

It was Pratte's last trip as a steamboat captain. There are indications that Pierre Chouteau was furious with the decisions made and not made by Pratte and Halsey, despite the profits. He bought Pratte out and demoted Halsey. Too late, the government sent vaccines to the upper Missouri.

Pratte invested time and energy in protecting his reputation, and it was successful. He was elected to the Missouri legislature and eventually became mayor of St. Louis. The *St. Peters*, it seems, was considered bad karma, bad medicine or just bad marketing for the company. Historian Michael M. Casler tells us it was dismantled in 1838.[45]

St. Peters was gone, but the results of its 1837 trip lingered on. The more nomadic tribes suffered less from smallpox. Nations that had seen smallpox more frequently had more people capable of caring for the sick, increasing

Like-a-Fishhook Village, the coalition city of the Mandan, Hidatsa and Arikara by Bears Arm. *State Historical Society of North Dakota.*

the patients' chance of survival. The Mandan and their only somewhat-less sedentary neighbors, the Hidatsa, had somehow been spared exposure for fifty-six years. Only senior citizens among their villages had been previously exposed. Only the least capable were available to help the young. Pregnancy was especially dangerous. So young women and children died, while women past fertility survived. Not only was there great death, population recovery would be impossible. It was a disaster of biblical proportions.

Chapter 11

JOSEPH LA BARGE

Historian Hiram Chittenden observed, in a region dependent on steamboat transportation, pilots and captains of steamboats "enjoyed exceptional opportunities of seeing and knowing the men who made the history of the Western country." In a career spanning more than half a century on the river, Joseph La Barge of St. Louis proved the truth of the remark.

Joseph La Barge went up the Missouri with a generation of fine artists: Catlin, Bodmer and Audubon. La Barge, at sixteen, was on the second voyage of the *Yellow Stone* to the upper Missouri in 1832 but only went as far as Council Bluffs. Artist and ethnographer George Catlin and fur trader Pierre Chouteau Jr. continued on to Fort Union. By the next year, La Barge was in command of the famous boat in a very trying emergency. In 1833, the *Yellow Stone* traveled in a two-boat fleet with the *Assiniboin* as far as Fort Pierre, where passengers, including German prince Maximilian of Wied and Swiss artist Karl Bodmer transferred over to the *Assiniboin* for the completion of the journey to Fort Union. The *Yellow Stone* loaded furs collected at Fort Pierre and returned to St. Louis. The season being not too far advanced, Captain Andrew Bennett loaded supplies and headed back upriver toward Council Bluffs.

A cholera epidemic sweeping the Missouri valley caught up with them. A clerk on the *Yellow Stone* under command of Captain Bennett, La Barge was one of the lucky survivors as cholera swept the boat, killing the pilot, most of the officers and so much of the crew that Bennett determined to moor the boat near the confluence of the Kansas and Missouri Rivers. He would personally travel to St. Louis to raise a relief crew, and in his absence, he no doubt reluctantly turned to young La Barge to care for the boat.

La Barge was not allowed to simply wait. Towns and camps tried to protect themselves from the epidemic by quarantine. The settlers of northwestern Missouri, knowing the boat carried cholera, sent a deputation to evict the *Yellow Stone* from the state. The seventeen-year-old acted as fireman, engineer and pilot. He got up steam and took the boat upriver, just beyond the state border. While acting as caretaker captain, La Barge saw the company's sister ship, *Assiniboin*, coming down the river. He signaled it his distress. Captain Bernard Pratte ignored his plea for help.

La Barge captained and piloted many other steamboats in a fifty-two-year career on the river. His career spanned nearly the entire history of steamboating on the Missouri and Yellowstone. Even when he was done traveling, his knowledge of the river was of value. The federal government paid him to create a list of steamboat wrecks on the Missouri.

A major figure in the brief golden age conjunction of steamboating and the fur trade, La Barge was twenty-seven when he piloted the *Omega* for Captain Joseph Sire in 1843. Sire, La Barge and the *Omega* set a speed record, taking only forty-nine days to reach Fort Union from St. Louis. Speed records had the effect of increasing the public esteem and marketability of those who set them. That run benefitted from high water. By comparison, an 1839 excursion from St. Louis only to Fort Pierre took sixty-three days to go one thousand miles fewer. Low water exposed so many sandbars and snags that the *Antelope* had to saw its way through. Passenger Joseph Nicollet wrote that the exposed trees, some rising as much as fifteen feet above the surface of the Missouri, were "like a forest of monsters armed with pikes and pitchforks."[46]

Snags were the major cause of wrecks for steamboats. Hiram Martin Chittenden estimated that 70 percent of boats lost were due to running into river debris. His figures don't quite hold for a later era, though they are in the same ballpark. In 1868, just under 10 percent of all 1,042 steamers working the Mississippi river system, including the Missouri and Ohio, were lost. Of that number, 53 percent were lost to sawyers and snags, and 40 percent burned or exploded. The remainder was destroyed in collisions with other boats.[47] Loss of life was rare in sinkings but much higher from boiler explosions.

The risk-reward was an essential part of business, often, but not always, insured against with business plans that still entailed extraordinary profit. Insurance on boats was considered to be double on the Missouri to the lower Mississippi, and that was considerable. William Lass puts premium rates at 12 percent of value for the boats themselves and nearly 8 percent for cargo on less dangerous streams.[48] Steamboats and the fur trade had economic consequences far beyond their own profits. Warehouses were built and stevedores hired, and white-collar jobs were created in management, marketing and complementary businesses. The story of the fur trade generally and steamboating in Dakota particularly is one of risk-taking entrepreneurs and fast-talking lobbyists who were often one and the same. The Chouteau family was premier among them, and throughout decades, one or another challenger engaged in trade and competition for government contracts.

La Barge worked for Pierre Chouteau Jr. from 1832 to 1840, tried his hand in opposition and worked again for and with the company over two more decades. In 1847, La Barge directed construction of a steamboat for his own use. *Martha* had only a two-foot draft carrying 180 tons. It was built with sturdy-bottom planks. It had two engines, an adaptation debuted by *Platte* on the Missouri in 1838. *Martha* was a side-wheeler. La Barge took his wife, Pelagie, along on its inaugural cruise, a visit to Fort Union. Pelagie La Barge is reputedly the first white woman to see its cottonwood walls.

On that 1847 trip, Pelagie and her captain had more excitement than they expected. *Martha* carried a new Indian agent and annuities for the Yankton and others. A messy situation evolved when the agent met the Yankton at Crow Creek, where a trading post was operated by Colin Campbell. The agent threw a feast and gave out some of the goods but stopped distribution of annuities short of completion, a fact apparent to the Yankton. The motive for stopping was to induce the recipients to travel upriver to Fort Pierre to receive the rest. The Yankton questioned why. There was no good answer but also no budging on the position.

Literal fuel was, figuratively, poured on the fire in a woodpile dispute. Campbell had prepared a woodpile for use by La Barge on his return trip. Seeing the hostility developing, the captain thought it prudent to put the wood on board immediately and set about to do it. The Yankton went on a sit-down strike, right on the woodpile, demanding to be paid before it could leave their bank. La Barge paid, but trouble was not averted.

When men from the boat tried to quickly load the wood, they were set on by braves, who used their rawhide horsewhips to disrupt the process. It took the intercession of Etienne Provost, a tough veteran of the river known and respected by the Yankton, to get the job done without further harassment.

But real trouble was on the way. High winds kept *Martha* moored throughout the day, and late in the afternoon, no doubt after a lot of discussion and planning, the Yankton overwhelmed the crew. La Barge heard the commotion and someone yell that deckhand Charles Smith had been killed. He rushed to Pelagie and detailed a passenger to stay with her and barricade her door with mattresses. La Barge then ran into Campbell, who told him the Yankton wanted the boat and its cargo. The crew and passengers would be free to go, if they did not resist, but otherwise no one would be spared.

La Barge wrote, "After the first rush the Indians seemed timorous and uncertain, evidently fearing some unpleasant surprise in the unknown labyrinths of the boat." He noted that they did have a knowledge of the workings of the steamboat, which they demonstrated by flooding the boilers at the first rush. *Martha* was dead in the water. La Barge recalled that he had a small cannon whose carriage was being repaired in the boiler room, and as the Yankton were largely only in possession of the front of the boat and its deck, he had the cannon hoisted through back channels, primed and loaded with boiler rivets. Revealing the cannon and himself, with lighted cigar in hand, La Barge had Campbell "tell them to get off the boat or I would blow them all to the devil."[49]

They got off very rapidly.

Pelagie was apparently not much shaken by the experience. She represented her gender and ethnicity to the Indians of the river, particularly creating a stir among the women. They examined "her with the liveliest interest, measuring her waist and the length of her hair, and wondering at the tastefulness and beauty of her dress....Several adopted her as their sister." La Barge reported that years after, on his trips up the river, these women would inquire about their white sister and send her presents. She always reciprocated. Thirty-eight years after meeting her, Pierre Garreau's daughter with an Arikara woman told La Barge that she remembered seeing Pelagie on that 1847 voyage.

The next year, Pelagie stayed home while La Barge took *Martha* up to Fort Union again. It was a sixty-five-day round trip notable for its return cargo. *Martha* carried not only furs and hides removed from animals but also live specimens, including buffaloes, elk, bears, antelopes and deer in pens and beavers in a large water tank.

La Barge had the good fortune to avoid economic loss from the great fire of 1849 that struck the wharves of St. Louis. His interest in *Martha*, which burned, ended after the 1848 season. He invested instead in building *St.*

Crowded levee in St. Louis. *Courtesy Special Collections, Murphy Library, University of Wisconsin–La Crosse.*

Ange. It was the first and perhaps the only boat built on the ways and launched with the boilers up and engines ready to turn the twin side-wheels as it hit water. It could carry 254 tons of cargo on its 170 feet of length by 28 feet of width.

It was on the occasion of *St. Ange*'s fancy-dan launching in mid-March that the *Missouri Daily Republican* of St. Louis editorialized, "There is no Captain on the Western waters more highly esteemed than Captain La Barge."

La Barge was operating *St. Ange* on May 17, returning late to St. Louis from delivering army goods to Fort Leavenworth. He was late because a storm forced a delay of several hours. It was a good thing.

The devastating fire started on the steamboat *White Cloud* about 10:00 p.m. and quickly spread to surrounding boats. Attempting to limit the damage, workers cut the ropes on burning boats, hoping to send them flaming harmlessly downstream to prevent spreading fire to the other boats on the wharves. It was a disastrous mistake. The first released boat, *Edward*

Bates', wouldn't behave. Wind drove it back to shore, drifting along the port, setting other boats on fire. In panicked response, workers determined to release unburning boats before *Bates'* reached them. Several were released but caught fire, and suddenly there was a fleet of burning ships out of control all along the waterfront. Fire spread to the business district, and by the time the fires were controlled, about nine hours after they started, St. Louis was devastated and the steamboat business wounded. The insurance settlements were instructive. Damage was estimated at $440,000 for the boats and their cargoes. Coverage was $225,000, but much of it was unpaid, as the insurance companies had insufficient capital and reserves to handle their exposure.[50] La Barge, on *St. Ange*, could see the glow of the fire as he approached St. Louis after midnight. At 1:00 a.m., he cruised the length of the city's burning waterfront looking for a berth before giving up and tying up at Bloody Island a safe distance across the river.

St. Ange and La Barge set a new speed record for St. Louis to Fort Union in 1850, making the trip, including stops at other posts in Dakota, in just twenty-eight days. The next year's trip was more difficult. Cholera was at large. *St. Ange* seemed to be a floating hospital, even a Jesuit hospital, complete with Father De Smet, known to the people of the West as the Black Robe; Father Christian Hoecken; and a physician on a science mission for the Smithsonian. The outbreak caused several deaths a day for a few days. It caused Father De Smet to ask Hoecken to hear his confession, but it was Hoecken who passed away and was buried by the mouth of the Little Sioux upriver from Council Bluffs.

In the drier, healthier Iowa air, La Barge ordered the boat emptied and cleaned, told the passengers to take a walk and had all the baggage aired. Reloaded, the boat proceeded. The epidemic receded.[51]

At the Grand River, the Arikara chief White Shield visited the boat because he had heard the Black Robe was on board and he had a favor to ask. While the lower Missouri was wet and malarial in 1851, there was drought in western Dakota. White Shield explained to La Barge, who understood Arikara because of its similarity to the Pawnee that the captain had learned at the beginning of his career in the fur trade, that the Arikara wanted Father De Smet to pray for rain.

Black Robe agreed and carried out the requested prayer with great solemnity and respect at the Arikara village. Then several of the Arikara visited the boat for lunch before returning home. That afternoon, a heavy thunderstorm unloaded on the gardens, villages, boat and all. De Smet mused, "They will think I did it. They will give me all the credit for it." That would certainly be a topic of conversation within the villages, but it was clear that French trapper and interpreter Pierre Garreau believed the good father knew the trick. He offered ten horses for the secret behind De Smet's effectiveness. Black Robe told him to be a good Christian and pray. Garreau held his horses.

Other activities in Dakota this trip were standard, but the year after setting a speed record, La Barge set a distance record, taking *St. Ange* one hundred miles beyond Fort Union, breaking a seventeen-year-old record set by *Assiniboin* in 1834.

Chapter 12

THE MORMON COW

Truth be told, we have no knowledge of the religious affiliation of the cow. But generations of commentators have referred to the incident with the Mormon cow that precipitated the Grattan massacre and subsequent walloping of the Brulé at Ash Hollow by General William "Mad Bear" Harney.

In 1854, an immigrant train of Mormons was nearing Fort Laramie when a cow wandered away from the train. It was found, killed and eaten by a Miniconjou, High Forehead, and his family. They were guests visiting Conquering Bear's band of Brulé. The Brulé, Miniconjou, Oglalla, Cheyenne and Arapaho had gathered in an unsustainable camp of six hundred lodges, where they were awaiting distribution of annuities. The treaty goods were late, and the camp was hungry.

The cow's Mormon owner considered it stolen by Indians and reported it so to the soldiers at Fort Laramie. Over a two-day period of discussions with Conquering Bear and demands made by the soldiers, agreement proved elusive. The military wanted to arrest High Forehead, and the cow's former owner wanted twenty-five dollars' compensation. Conquering Bear would not arrest a guest from another band or allow him to be arrested. Cash money was not available to the Brulé, but other valuable compensation was offered and rejected.

The young Second Lieutenant John Grattan thought to bring home the government's demands by entering Conquering Bear's camp with thirty men and two field pieces. The conversation didn't go well. Conquering Bear was the first and only Indian fatality. Grattan and every man in his unit were killed almost instantly.

After the Grattan affair, Sioux poured into the Fort Pierre area, advocating for a general war against the United States, but significantly, they were doing that at a post where annuities were distributed. Even before that, there had been unrest. Hunkpapa and Blackfeet Sioux had refused annuities. Their agent said they preferred "war and stealing horses to receiving presents." Fort Union was troubled by a group of about sixty Sioux who killed a worker and stole twenty-six horses.

Other practical chiefs in the winter of 1853–54 found the weather too warm to cluster buffalo in the wooded river bottoms, forcing hunters to go farther for fewer. They asked that the government respond with more food and fewer other things. They could trade what buffalo robes they had accumulated for cloth and metal tools. In early July, Agent Alfred Vaughn was able to distribute good at Fort Union to nine of the thirteen tribes in his region. Hunkpapa and Blackfeet resisters threatened those who were accepting of the 1851 Fort Laramie Treaty. Vaughn reported that the Mandan, Hidatsa and Arikara wanted the United States to order 150 well-armed, uniformed soldiers to "give those Black Feet and Uncpapas a good whipping."

After the Grattan event in August, things got even more tense. At Fort Pierre in November, Vaughn tried to give the Blackfeet and Hunkpapa things other than a good whipping. He offered food and, counterintuitively, some ammunition. The response from a Lakota named Red Leaf was dramatic. He drew a huge knife, cut every sack of goods and "scattered the contents in every direction he then threw the Tobacco Powder and Balls in the River and in quick succession forty or fifty guns was fired off all around and about me." It was an impressive display of strength and confidence. We don't need your gifts or even your ammunition, Red Leaf demonstrated.

The war was on, but the traders and the government pursued separate courses. While General "Mad Bear" Harney organized a punitive expedition, agents continued to operate trading posts in what had become a war zone. In February 1855, three hundred Hunkpapa and Blackfeet attacked Assiniboine camped by Fort Union, disrupting the trade. At Fort Clark, seven months later, the Lakota didn't kill anyone but once again intimidated Agent Vaughn and destroyed presents he tried to dispense to the Indians. That winter, the Yanktonnai Dakota joined in the intimidation. Their leader Big Head went to Fort Clark with eighty warriors to get their annuities. Vaughn threw a feast, but it did not pacify Big Head, who abused the agent by grabbing his glasses and demanding to be taken to the storeroom to see what goods might be there. Surrounded by six armed Yanktonnai, Vaughn endured insults while warriors in the compound shot at unlucky chickens and a lucky cat. The intimidation was enough for Big Head. They left the traders and the agent without a scratch.

Vaughn didn't take it well. He wanted Big Head and one-third of the nearby Hunkpapa and Blackfeet Sioux exterminated. He didn't get his wish, but General Harney devastated the Brulé and Oglalla under Blue Thunder at Ash Hollow, September 3, and marched his troops to Fort Pierre for the winter, open to peace negotiations with all the nations of the region. Some parts of the vast, anarchic confederacy that was the Great Sioux Nation agreed to peace, but others ignored Harney. One of the Hunkpapa leaders Harney found cooperative was Bear's Rib.[52] He'd been so for some time. In 1851, Fort Pierre's bourgeois Honoré Picotte was annoyed when an Indian had killed one of the fort's cows. He believed the Indian had no interest in or no way of compensating the company for its minor loss, but he couldn't let it go. Picotte decided to mutter in a place that might get some results. Bear's Rib was in the fort watching some of the workmen. One of those was Louis Dace Letellier, who wrote about the scene:

> *Boss Picotte was passing nearby, his head hanging low, his hands behind his back as usual, talking to himself in a tone loud enough to be heard by the chief.*
>
> *"Where is the time," he was saying, "when there were brave men in the Sioux nation. Alas, that time is past. The cowards don't fear anything now. They are all chiefs, they kill our cattle and the braves of today dare not punish the guilty ones."*
>
> *The chief's smiling face took a sudden somber cunning appearance. Without saying a word, he walked out of the fort. He went and inquired who among the men in his camp had killed any cattle belonging to the fort. Someone told him who it was that had killed a cow. He went for his gun and proceeded to the lodge of the guilty one, walked in, and* [said,] *"Comrade, I have come to kill you."*[53]

Bear's Rib made good his pledge.

Chapter 13

WAR WITH THE SIOUX

In 1866, Fort Union was torn down and the robe trade further reduced. Military occupation and offensives took its place. Fort Buford and the Thirteenth Infantry, actually and symbolically, replaced Fort Union, the multinational center of peaceful commerce.

The explosion in southern Minnesota in August 1862 called the Dakota Uprising cast a scatter pattern to the farthermost reaches of Dakota, but it didn't greatly affect the nearby Yankton. By the late 1850s, pressure to open up what is now southeastern South Dakota to white settlement had become very strong. The Yankton leader *Padaniapapi*, Struck-by-the-Ree, determined that negotiating with the Americans was superior to armed resistance. Struck-by-the-Ree and several other Yankton headmen journeyed to Washington, D.C., in late 1857 to negotiate a treaty with the federal government. For more than three and a half months, they worked out the terms of a treaty of land cession. Struck-by-the-Ree's name appears first on the Treaty of Washington, signed April 19, 1858. Other signators for the Yankton were Black Bear, Medicine Crow, White Swan, Pretty Boy, Feather in the Ear, Crazy Bull and Frank Deloria.

Returning from Washington, Struck-by-the-Ree told his people, "The white men are coming in like maggots. It is useless to resist them. They are many more than we are. We could not hope to stop them. Many of our brave warriors would be killed, our women and children left in sorrow, and still we would not stop them. We must accept it, get the best terms we can get and try to adopt their ways."[54]

For about 11.5 million acres, a payment of approximately $1.6 million in annuities was to be paid over the next fifty years. Specific provisions of the treaty called for educating the tribe to develop skills in agriculture, industrial arts and homemaking. The treaty provided for the removal of the Yankton to a 475,000-acre reservation on the north side of the Missouri River in what is now Charles Mix County. (Charles E. Mix was the commissioner who signed for the federal government.) The U.S. Senate ratified the treaty on February 16, 1859, and President Buchanan authorized it ten days later. On July 10, 1859, the Yankton Sioux vacated the ceded lands and moved onto the newly created reservation.

With the shelling of Fort Sumter, the Civil War began on April 12, 1861. It had clear and not-so-clear effects. It appears to have strengthened the voices of armed resistance by Indians from Arizona to Minnesota. Simultaneously, it was more difficult for the United States to live up to its treaty commitments, further alienating the Indian nations.

Between the war and increasingly hostile actions along the river, steamboats started holding drills for passengers to defend the boats from Rebels or Indians.

In May 1862, the docks in St. Louis were filled with men eager to get to the gold fields in Montana. Steamboats could get them all the way to Fort Benton, where they could provision themselves for prospecting. The American Fur Company was happy to sell the tickets. But there was more trouble in the air between the United States and the Sioux council fires, as the miners boarded the *Spread Eagle* and the *Key West*.

The alleged proximate cause of a grievance by the Sioux were shortages in the annuities promised in the peace negotiations after General Harney's punitive campaign. When the *Spread Eagle* arrived at Fort Pierre, the scene was distressing. Hundreds of Sioux warriors in a bad mood met the steamboat. They accused the fur company of stealing goods meant as gifts and turning them into trade goods. But the real issue appears to have had more to do with pride and general anger toward the United States than with the annuities, which were refused by every band and headman other than the Hunkpapa Bear's Rib. While taking the treaty goods, Bear's Rib told Agent Samuel Latta that he would be in danger. The other bands of Sioux wouldn't like it, and he might be killed. He was, though it wasn't certain it had to do with the annuities.

As the boat made its way north, Sans Arc and Miniconjou warriors, 150 strong, came to Fort Pierre with a mission. They declared their hostility to not just the Americans but to any collaborators. When Bear's Rib challenged them, one of the Sans Arc let fly a fatal arrow. The harsh rhetoric and actions reflected a widespread attitude among the entire greater Sioux Nation.

In August, in Minnesota, the Wahpeton, Mdewaukan and Wahpekute bands of Dakota were also suffering on their two reserves, the upper and lower agencies. Crop failure in 1861 meant a long, hungry winter. Spring is always the hungriest time on the northern plains. The first break in the cycle would be delivery of annuities, including cash with which to purchase food from agency shopkeepers. That was typically provided in June, but in 1862, it was delayed. Five thousand Mdewaukan assembled in mid-July at Yellow Medicine to demand release of goods being held at the upper agency. They received them. On the lower agency, things were similar. The small military detachments, stretched thin by the Civil War, recognized their vulnerability in a general uprising and encouraged distribution of food, but while the government owed cash to the Dakota, local merchants resisted offering credit. Shopkeeper Andrew Myrick is reputed to have said, "If they are hungry, let them eat grass."[55]

Pointless murders committed by young Wahpekute on August 17 sparked a war. The elder chiefs counseled peace while less cautious warriors called for a general uprising. Little Crow's leadership was sought by Big Eagle, Mankato, Wabasha and Traveling Hail, but he was angry with the loud voices calling for war. He lectured:

> *Braves, you are like little children; you know not what you are doing. You are full of the Whiteman's devil water. You are like dogs in the hot moon, when they run mad and snap at their own shadows. We are only little herds of buffaloes left scatter; the great herds that once covered the prairies are no more. See! The Whitemen are like the locusts, when they fly so thick that the whole sky is a snowstorm. You may kill one, two, ten, yes, as many as the leaves in the forest yonder, and their brothers will not miss them. Kill one, two, ten, and ten times ten will come to kill you. Count your fingers all day long and Whiteman with guns in their hands will come faster than you can count.*[56]

Hopeless or not, the urge to war was irresistible. The chiefs, led by Little Crow, accepted leadership in a war they considered hopeless. Hundreds of settlers and Indians were killed. Myrick ended up dead with a mouthful of grass. The citizens of New Ulm fought in the streets from barricades as 190 buildings burned. Fort Ridgely was nearly overrun, but the old chiefs were right. It was hopeless. Little Crow died, and hundreds of Dakota were taken prisoner and sentenced to hang. Abraham Lincoln commuted the sentences of all but thirty-two, who died in the largest mass hanging in the United States. The United States restored dominance in Minnesota, but it wasn't enough to satisfy the desire for vengeance by those Minnesotans terrorized by the uprising. Two policies were deployed in 1863 to calm the whites and punish the Indians.

Removal of Indians from southern Minnesota was the policy intended to provide a calming influence. The Dakota would be moved to Dakota, lock, stock and barrel. An Indian nation that had sat out the uprising, the Winnebago, or Ho-Chunk, was also expelled. Their crime was being nonwhite and in possession of prime farmland. On February 21, 1863, Congress delighted the citizens of Mankato, Minnesota, and surroundings by ordering the Winnebago, who had already been forced from Illinois and Wisconsin, to be moved from their fertile farms near the Crow Wing River to the more arid Crow Creek by Fort Thompson in Dakota.

The Winnebago removal is indicative of something important. It had to be because it was such an expensive and inhumane way to conduct the movement of two thousand people over 300 miles. Wagons and mules could have easily carried the possessions and invalid members of the Winnebago community. Instead, these people, who had been neutral during the recent conflict around them, were forced onto steamboats at Mankato on the Minnesota River and steamed to the Mississippi at Fort Snelling. Then they were taken down the Mississippi to the Missouri and finally back up the Missouri to Fort Thompson. It was weeks of confinement and a 1,900-mile taxpayer-funded consignment of human cargo. Many died.

In 1863, twin punitive expeditions were launched into Dakota. General Henry Sibley fought engagements from Big Mound on the central plains of Dakota, right up to the Missouri near Apple Creek. He'd hoped to meet General Alfred Sully there. He was supposed to have a steamboat armada with troops and supplies waiting, but the Missouri was extremely low that summer; Sully's boats never arrived. The Sioux warriors, including Sitting Bull, who counted coup in an attempt to drive off Sibley's livestock in a fight at Dead Buffalo Lake, fought a delaying action while women and children slipped across the Missouri. The last fighters swam across to their people under fire and then turned and returned fire from the safety of Morton County, probably pretty close to where Fort Lincoln would stand a decade later.

In 1863, La Barge carried two Indian agents and annuities to Dakota on *Robert Campbell*. At Fort Pierre, trouble began. Agent Samuel Latta was very bad at his job. He had so angered the Sioux previously that he had been ordered never to come back. Now he was back to anger them some more.

Latta shorted the Sioux bands, holding back one-third of their annuities. The bands knew La Barge and asked him to intercede. He was helpless. The Sioux promised to follow the boat and cause trouble. They kept their promise. It was a remarkable, marathon performance, really; whenever *Robert Campbell* stopped for wood over hundreds of miles, La Barge found hostile Sioux waiting. Between stops, at any convenient point of land, snipers took aim at the boat, which La Barge made fortress-like, using the cargo for protection. All the passengers were armed.

On July 7, La Barge was told by an advance hunter that 1,500 Sioux were waiting at Tobacco Gardens, a spot where the channel is narrow between Fort Berthold and Fort Union. As the boat approached the danger zone, eagle-eyed Natawista, traveling with her husband, Alexander Culbertson, noticed movement on a ridge. Then everyone saw two hundred Hunkpapa, Miniconjou and Blackfeet Lakota across the boat's path. La Barge anchored for a conversation.

The Lakota simply wanted their annuities. They buried their tomahawks in the sand. Agent Latta wanted to talk. They invited him to come across in a boat. La Barge and Natawista argued against it. She said it was a trap and that other warriors would suddenly appear from the brush if they took *Robert Campbell* to shore. Latta wanted several chiefs to come on board, and they agreed to do so, if he came to escort them. Latta agreed and against his better judgment, La Barge allowed a crew to volunteer to row Latta over in a yawl. The volunteers stepped forward, but Latta lost his enthusiasm for the project, went to his cabin and feigned illness.

Of the seven men sent in the yawl, three were killed and one seriously wounded as soon as they landed. The well-armed boat sent small arms and howitzer fire raking the shore. The Lakota taunted the people on the boat, urging them to come out and fight on the shore. The boat replied with three howitzers and an array of guns. After three hours and eighteen Indians killed, the Lakota withdrew, and the boat went on to Fort Union.

Sully did get his steamboats into the fight the next year, building and supplying Fort Rice in 1864, before heading off to the Battle of the Killdeer Mountains. A reporter from St. Paul captured an important moment in the history of steamboats and relations between the United States and the Indian nations.

The steamboat *Yellowstone*—a different one, the first one had long ago gone downriver to where it became the boat the saved Texas according to

Fort Rice, established 1864 by General Alfred Sully. *Courtesy Fort Abraham Lincoln Foundation.*

Sam Houston, but that's another story—stopped at the construction site of Fort Rice on its way from Fort Berthold. It was hauling thousands of buffalo hides and meat was hanging all around the decks to dry.

The reporter captured the contradictions—the conflict between trade and conquest both fueled by steam. He wrote:

> *Some 100 lodges of Sioux were encamped on the river opposite Berthold, who crossed by the boat to dispose of their robes at the post, for goods.*
>
> *It is not a little singular that trade is permitted with those Indians, supplying their wants and necessities, while the Government is endeavoring at such a tremendous expense to bring them to terms.*
>
> *Passengers say that these Missouri Fur Companies need watching.*

Grant Prince Marsh was a mate on one of Sully's boats, the *Marcella*. It was his first trip to the upper Missouri, where he would carve a legendary career.

Sully's armada included eight steamboats, two of which went up the Yellowstone to provide much-appreciated support to haggard troops who had struggled through the Bad Lands under constant and deadly guerrilla harassment. The *Marcella* went upriver to attempt to stay as close as possible to Sully's two-thousand-man army as it struck northwest toward *Takahokuty*, the place where they take the deer and site of what history calls the Battle of the Killdeer Mountains. At the future site of Bismarck, Grant Marsh and some crew members went ashore to investigate some metal and debris. They concluded that this was the site of the crossing of the main body of Sioux escaping General Sibley's punishment in 1863 and named it Wagon Wheel Bluff. The site later housed an Indian school, which morphed into the North Dakota National Guard's Fraine Barracks.

The *Island City*, *Alone* and *Chippewa Falls* were dispatched to the Yellowstone River. *Island City* snagged and sunk. The others did important duty at the close of Sully's campaign.

A remarkable forty-seven-mile walk on a hot July day on the plains brought Sully's cannon, cavalry and infantry to the base of the two large, flat-topped buttes that form the Killdeer Mountains, rising up to one thousand feet above the prairie. It was the largest military engagement ever held on the northern plains. The five thousand gathered Lakota and Dakota would have seen the dust of Sully's column for most of the day, July 27. Strong in numbers with leaders like Sitting Bull, Gall and Inkpaduta, they were ready to defend their homeland, and they had the advantage of elevation. Whether it was considered by the war leaders or not, the advantage that came into play most effectively was the proximity to the Bad Lands.

The Sioux had never faced a fight like the one on July 28 at Killdeer. Sully held tight discipline on his men as they marched steadily toward the tepees gathered above them. It was an open-square formation, with cavalry dismounted and cannon protected in the middle of the square. The warriors were not well armed, though they were well mounted. Every taunting act of personal bravery attempting to draw the soldiers into breaking discipline was ignored. The square moved relentlessly forward to the point that cannon fire could reach the spectators at the tepees. At that point, the battle devolved into a delaying action by the warriors while the women and children fled with whatever they could, over the mountains and down into the Little Missouri Bad Lands.

After burning all the food, belongings and tepees, Sully followed the Sioux into the narrow ravines and tangled country that he dubbed "hell with the fires put out." He spent a miserable, dangerous and nearly disastrous month of August extricating himself from the Bad Lands, struggling constantly under threat of ambush and guerrilla fighters, who struck without warning and disappeared before Sully's cannon and superior firearms could be brought to bear.[57] Rather than following the Little Missouri's tortured course north and east to its meeting with the Missouri, Sully instead set out for the Yellowstone to the west.

The first steamboat to ascend the Yellowstone was the light-draft *Chippewa Falls*. Sully's men heard its whistle on the high plains calling back and forth with *Alone* trailing fifty or so miles behind. Near what became Glendive, the boats met the soldiers. The steamboats carried Sully's distressed army up to the Big Opening, the Yellowstone's flat floodplain on the west bank of the river, and finally helped them cross to the north bank of the Missouri near Fort Union.[58]

The punitive expeditions ended there. The following years saw growth and consolidation of American military power into the region, and not coincidentally, much of that was along the Missouri River, where it could be supplied by steamboats. Fort Rice was made permanent. Fort Buford's soldiers used some wood from dismantling Fort Union in 1866, a striking symbol of the change that had taken place. Fort Stevenson was built between the two in 1867.

From Sitting Bull's point of view, the battle at the Killdeer Mountains and the ensuing campaign in the Bad Lands taught valuable lessons. Prime among them was that his people needed to be better armed, and so old animosities with the Metis and Chippewa would be overlooked to facilitate the arms trade. Where he had traded at Fort Union, Sitting Bull hated the trading fort being replaced by the military's Fort Buford in 1866. It was a constant insult to the Hunkpapa in the heart of some of the best remaining buffalo prairie.

Red Cloud and the Oglalla felt that way about Fort Phil Kearny on the Bozeman Trail, also built in 1866. It was besieged from the time it was built. The most significant battle in Red Cloud's War was the Fetterman fight, where eighty-one soldiers marched out of Fort Kearny to engage Crazy Horse and none marched back in.

The U.S. Army was stretched thin after the Civil War. It shrank in size dramatically at the same time it was asked to occupy the former Confederate states and deal with Indian resistance to immigration and transportation from the southern plains to Canada. The Pony Express, telegraph and the Union Pacific on the central and southern plains were easier to disrupt than steamboat traffic on the northern.

Much as it galled War Department chief General William Tecumseh Sherman, practical considerations on the limits of power made him choose where to fight. While he advocated destruction of buffalo herds to diminish the Indian's "larder" and urged killing Indian children because "nits make lice," the general accepted that it was more in the national interest that the southern plains be brought under control than the northern plains. That could come later.

The Fort Laramie Treaty of 1868 ensued. It accepted Red Cloud's victory; closed the Bozeman Trail forts; created the great Sioux reservation west of the Missouri, including the Black Hills, *Paha Sapa*; and barred whites from entering the Powder River country of Wyoming and Montana. Sitting Bull, not in attendance, had sent word of his opposition to peace because it didn't close Forts Stevenson and Buford and steamboats would still travel through Hunkpapa country.

In a follow-up conference at Fort Rice with Hunkpapa representatives and peace commissioners, including Sully and Harney, Gall reiterated what Sitting Bull had earlier said in opposition to the Fort Laramie treaty they wanted no forts and no steamboats above Fort Rice. "If we sign this peace treaty," Gall said to Father DeSmet, "then the steamboats must stop traveling up our river. The forts above Ft. Rice must be closed and burnt." Gall, as Red Cloud had, must have believed the forts would be. He signed the treaty. The forts were not burned. Sitting Bull was elected to an unprecedented position of authority by a multi-Lakota band council of resistance in 1869. Gall joined him in attacking Fort Buford. Steamboats did not quit running the river, and other forts were built, including Fort Abraham Lincoln in 1872.

St. Louis lost the upper Missouri business in this period. Chicago grabbed a big piece of it when rails from there touched the Missouri at Omaha in 1867, Sioux City in 1868 and Yankton and Bismarck in 1873. Each of those had a moment as a major port for the Montana trade, with Bismarck, farthest upriver, outlasting all the rest.

Railroads were the key factor in a game of river port leapfrog. Sioux City becomes head of navigation in 1868, with the Chicago and Northwestern Railroad. The first train arrived there on March 14, 1868. It had competition from a far west railhead completed in Corinne, Utah, in 1869, but it was the farthest point up the Missouri that touched rails.

Chapter 14

STEAMING THE RED RIVER

The first "port city" in Dakota was not on the Missouri. The Northern Pacific reached Fargo in 1872, and half a decade of regular steamboat traffic between Fargo, Grand Forks and Winnipeg ensued. The conjunction between steamboats and railroads in Dakota follows a pattern. Steamboats carry equipment and supplies to support railroad construction. Then, access to railheads improves steamboat business from those railheads. Then completion of the rail network kills steamboating.

The first steamboat on the Red was a commercial experiment by the St. Paul Chamber of Commerce. St. Paul, on the Mississippi, and Winnipeg, at the confluence of the Red and Assiniboine, had long carried on commerce. Oxcart trails ran the ridges above glacial Lake Agassiz parallel along the Red River from Winnipeg–St. Boniface and then southeast to St. Cloud, Fort Snelling and St. Paul. The origins of the route are obscure but after the founding of Fort Snelling in 1819, the traffic, already well established, became frequent.

In 1858, the St. Paul Chamber recruited Anson Northrup, a veteran Mississippi River captain, to build a steamboat on the Red that would replace a large portion of the oxcart trails. His incentive was a $2,000 reward for completion of the effort. Northrup chose a construction spot on the east bank, opposite the mouth of the Sheyenne River, at a now-vanished site known as Lafayette, a few miles north of what would become Fargo.

Northrup steamed his *North Star* from the Mississippi to the Crow Wing River and up the Crow Wing to the mouth of the Gull River. There he chopped it up and moved it in an incredible effort over winter trails and trails of Northrup's forces' own making. The boiler alone weighed more than five tons. The caravan included seventeen teams of horses, thirteen yoke of oxen and thirty men.

The boat, renamed *Anson Northrup*, was reassembled in the spring, launched on the Red and immediately headed for Winnipeg. It arrived to cannons firing, bells ringing and crowd approval. The boat's namesake chose not to be its operator. Perhaps he wasn't completely happy with his Mississippi River steamer on the narrower Red. It was a three-deck stern-wheeler with four staterooms that could be shared by up to twelve ladies and a common room with twenty-four berths separated only by curtains. Only the pilothouse, according to an unhappy passenger, allowed access to cooling breezes. The boiler smokestack ran right through the main cabin, which was always heated. That would not be appreciated in the heart of the Red's navigation season. Other observers, including its own pilot didn't give it much respect.

A reporter for the Winnipeg-based *Nor'-Wester* described the large boat's handling on the narrow Red, "The boat has such an extraordinary affection for the shore that at times no amount of rudder and wheel can cure her headstrong and landward fancies." Captain C.P.V. Lull said it was "nothing better than a lumbering old pine-basket, Sir, which you have to handle as gingerly as a hamper of eggs."

Anson Northrup, renamed *Pioneer*, suffered a freak death before the navigation season of 1862. Tied up taut near Fort Garry, the boat tipped after a sudden drop in the Red, took on water and sank in nine feet of water. Efforts to raise the boat failed.

Another steamboat was already planned for the Red, so there still was at least a partial navigation season in 1862. An 1860 effort to steam *Freighter* from the Mississippi to the Red had ended in failure above Big Stone Lake. It was theoretically possible to steam on a spring flood across the low continental divide between Big Stone Lake and Lake Traverse, from which the Bois de Sioux River emanates and eventually becomes the Red when it meets the Ottertail River by Wahpeton-Breckenridge. The typical head of navigation on the Red was still far downstream at Georgetown, below the mouth of the Sheyenne, but in spring, hope springs eternal.

Freighter over-wintered in Big Stone Lake and set out with the spring snowmelt. It went far enough to get into real trouble. Grounded in shallow water that became no water, *Freighter* became a relic on the prairie. Like *North Star*, it was cannibalized and its machinery hauled overland to the Red. Christened *International*, its best moments were among its first. At a substantial 137 by 26 feet, its arrival at Fort Garry on May 26, 1862, was, to the *Nor'-Wester*, "a really grand affair. Its size and finish would make it respectable even amid the finest floating palaces of the Mississippi."

It was a bad time to launch a new steamboat enterprise on the Red. Water levels were low in the latter half of the summer, and the Minnesota Uprising was about to explode. *International* spent most of the 1863 season docked at Fort Abercrombie to avail itself of the protection of the fort's guns and soldiers. Fort Abercrombie had been besieged for six weeks the previous fall, and angry Dakota Indians were still active along the Red. In 1864, *International* was sold to the Hudson's Bay Company, which had a negative view of increased settlement damaging its fur trade. It ran only sporadically through 1870.

A second era of steamboating on the Red opened with the 1870s and closed within a decade. Alexander Griggs and James J. Hill, both thirty-two years old in 1870, formed Hill, Griggs and Company of St. Paul. Hill would become the "Empire Builder," as the fabulously wealthy head of the Great Northern Railway and other enterprises. Griggs would become the founder of Grand Forks, an enterprising booster and business leader of the city and its mayor.

Griggs was a steamboat pilot on the Mississippi out of his boyhood home of St. Paul at age nineteen. He ran boats there until he and Hill combined enterprises. Griggs supervised construction of *Selkirk* on the east bank of the Red thirty miles south of Moorhead at McCauleyville and began running goods between Fort Garry and sites upriver in 1871.

That same year, the first Northern Pacific track reached Moorhead, and steamboats could connect the growing Manitoba province with the world through the intercontinental railroad system of the United States. It was a boom era, and Griggs and Hill did very well. The Hudson's Bay Company saw *Selkirk* and potential for profit and dusted off *International* for full-time service.

Hill and HBC found a way to avoid competition. Hill sold *Selkirk* to HBC, which then placed its two steamboats under the management of the Red River Transportation Company, which was essentially Hill, Griggs and Company. The company hired Norman Kittson, HBC's shipping agent for its Red River business, as manager. Within a short time, Kittson had five steamboats running between Fort Garry and Moorhead. The trip took three to five days. It was not typically dangerous. Boats could operate from ice out to freezing, typically a season from April through October.

Business was good for the steamboat company as Winnipeg did not get rail service until the end of 1878. It got its first railroad engine in October 1877. It did not come on rails. It did come by efforts of *Selkirk*. The engine,

Alexander Griggs statue on Grand Forks County lawn. Griggs was a steamboat captain and one of the founders of Grand Forks. *Photo by the author.*

named Countess of Dufferin, was loaded onto barges at Fisher's Landing on the Red Lake River along with a caboose and six flatcars. *Selkirk* pushed the barges down the Red Lake to the Red and on to St. Boniface, the French-Metís city across the Red from Winnipeg. *Selkirk* arrived on October 9, 1877, carrying, as it were, the seeds of its own irrelevance.

Much more than the steamboat company titans on the Missouri, Hill and Kittson, particularly, on the Red made an effortless transition to railroads. The Panic of 1873 drove the St. Paul and Pacific Railroad into bankruptcy. Hill put together a group of investors, including Kittson, bought the St. Paul and Pacific and expanded its reach. Renamed the St. Paul, Minneapolis and Manitoba Railway, its line connected St. Paul and the world with Dominion City, Manitoba, on December 3, 1878.

Red River port for Grandin Line elevator. *Courtesy Special Collections, Murphy Library, University of Wisconsin–La Crosse.*

The Countess of Dufferin was there, the countess having gone to work in building the Pembina Branch from St. Boniface toward the border.

Hill and Kittson became wealthy, and the company poured its profits into further acquisitions and expansions that eventually became Hill's transcontinental Great Northern Railway.

Steamboat operations faded in relevance alongside their profits. Boats found a reason to exist up to 1912, and new boats were built on the Red—two in 1878, when the writing should have been on the wall about rail service supplanting steamboats, and one each in 1881 and 1895. *J.L. Grandin*, 1878, and *Grand Forks*, 1895, were in the business of shipping grain from riverside facilities. C.H. Alsop picked up a boat inadequate for the Mississippi, had it disassembled and then had it reassembled on the Red as *Pluck* in 1878. In 1881, he had *Alsop* built. Both boats were triple-deckers with a cabin deck, *Alsop's* being the more extensive.

Between the construction of Alsop's two boats, the *International* ended its career in 1880. Fargo-Moorhead lost regular steamboat service in 1886. *Alsop* ended its career the same year. *Grandin* got swept away by the flood of 1897 and ended up in a field near Halstad, Minnesota. In Grand Forks, steamboats found business up to 1910. The last two boats on the river were both lost in 1912. *Grand Forks* and *Fram* each sank that year.

Griggs is a county in North Dakota, and Griggs Landing is an interpretive rest area on I-29. Kittson is a street in Grand Forks and a county in Minnesota.

STEAMBOATS OF THE RED RIVER OF THE NORTH[59]

DATE IN SERVICE	STEAMBOAT NAME	CONSTRUCTION SITE
1859	*Anson Northrup/Pioneer*	Lafayette, Minnesota
1862	*International*	Georgetown, Minnesota
1871	*Selkirk*	McCauleyville, Minnesota
1872	*Dakota*	Breckenridge, Minnesota
1874	*Alpha*	Breckenridge, Minnesota
1874	*Cheyenne*	Grand Forks, Dakota Territory
1875	*Manitoba*	Moorhead, Minnesota
1875	*Minnesota*	Moorhead, Minnesota
1878	*J.L. Grandin*	Fargo, Dakota Territory
1878	*Pluck*	Moorhead, Minnesota
1882	*H.W. Alsop*	Moorhead, Minnesota
1890	*Fram*	East Grand Forks, Minnesota
1895	*Grand Forks*	Grand Forks, North Dakota

Chapter 15

A TALE OF TWO CITIES

Yankton and Bismarck

When the Dakota Southern rolled into Yankton on February 3, 1873, the Missouri River in Dakota had its first railhead. Bismarck was just months behind.

In 1873, Yankton was the capital of Dakota Territory and had been so for eleven years. It was platted and occupied immediately following the treaty of 1859 with the Yankton Sioux. Subsequent to the treaty signing and removal of the Yankton people from Yankton, local boosters began arguing for territorial status. Particularly important in that lobbying effort was John Blair Smith Todd, army veteran of the Mexican War and former commander at Fort Ripley. Todd resigned his commission in September 1856 and took a position as post sutler at Fort Randall. Todd and partner Daniel Frost went into business as independents necessarily in opposition to the dominant Missouri Fur Company. Todd and Frost began selling groceries in Sioux City and opened a trading post at the mouth of the James in 1857 and one at the Vermillion in 1858. Todd moved to Yankton after the treaty, became its most prominent citizen and an effective advocate for the creation of Dakota, which was created by an act of Congress two days before Abraham Lincoln was sworn in as president. Lincoln appointed his friend, and personal doctor, state senator William A. Jayne as the first governor of Dakota Territory.

The proposed territory had far more members of Indian nations than U.S. citizens. There were about three hundred people in Yankton, three hundred in Pembina who were mostly Metís and just a scattering of dozens of others at small settlements along the Missouri. Jayne declared Yankton the temporary capital of Dakota, pending official action by the first legislative assembly. An election in September 1861 named the legislators, and they came together the following March. It also sent Todd to Washington as territorial delegate to Congress.

The choice of Yankton as territorial capital, though logical, was not without controversy. Bon Homme and Vermillion competed with Yankton for the choice. Todd got into the battle in a big way, at one point throwing the Speaker of the House through a closed window. Governor Jayne provided military protection for the rest of the debate.

In an essay on William Jayne, D. Jerome Tweton quotes an observer of the contest, saying, "A little blood was shed, much whiskey drunk, a few eyes blackened, revolvers drawn, and some running done."

Yankton won. It would remain territorial capital until 1883, when the Northern Pacific worked with boosters in the northern half of the territory to move the capital to Bismarck.

In 1873, Yankton had political, social and cultural advantages over the rough new city of Bismarck, known as the "Wickedest City in the West." Bismarck's Bloody Fourth Street saloons and shootings made Deadwood seem tame and civilized.[60] So while Bismarck had a clear, seven-hundred-mile advantage over Yankton in reaching the upper Missouri, the principals of steamboat companies serving that region often chose Yankton as their homes. That advantage faded as Bismarck became more established and less bloody. Yankton could compete economically in terms of which city was better situated for access to the Black Hills and was natural for access to Fort Pierre and Fort Randall, but trade with settlements and trading posts in the Yellowstone valley and upper Missouri were to Bismarck's advantage.

The rise of Bismarck was dictated by geography and the Northern Pacific Railroad. The competition in Yankton was homegrown. Leading figures in commerce in Yankton lobbied for territorial status and rail service. Failing to encourage an established rail company to connect to Yankton and unable to get federal land grants for railways as had the Northern Pacific, local business leaders organized the Dakota Southern Railroad to connect Yankton with rails sixty miles to the east. The territorial legislature quite naturally favored the project and authorized the issuance of bonds by Yankton County and private commitments by Judge W.W. Brookings and J.M. Stone, who reportedly mortgaged their holdings to aid expansion of rail service.

Bismarck's role as the winner of the leapfrog game may have been so short-lived as to discourage the city's development as an inland port, but macroeconomics intervened. The financial Panic of 1873 halted construction of the transcontinental line although survey crews continued into Montana, accompanied by George Custer and the Seventh Cavalry, who fought Hunkpapa along the Big Horn River in 1873 and again, more famously, in 1876 at the Battle of Little Big Horn.

Fargo was reached by the Northern Pacific in 1872, and its construction teams raced across the prairie to the Missouri. Steamboats under Walter Burleigh carried road-grading equipment to the Crossing, the projected place where a bridge would carry the Northern Pacific into Montana and beyond. His commission from the railroad was to grade fifty miles of roadbed from the Crossing toward a meeting with the line coming from Fargo.

Burleigh's *Miner* loaded at the Sioux City railhead and transported his equipment, laborers and sustenance to the spot that would be the seat of the county bearing his name and, eventually, the capital city of North Dakota.

WALTER A. BURLEIGH

Born: October 25, 1820, Waterville, Maine
Died: March 7, 1896, Yankton, South Dakota

In his first days in the White House, Abraham Lincoln appointed Walter Burleigh Indian agent to the Yankton Sioux. He was accused by the Yankton of short-changing them for personal gain, but corruption didn't bring down many of those with strong Republican connections in those decades. In 1865, he was elected to represent Dakota Territory in Congress, and his father-in-law was appointed governor of Dakota.

Burleigh was a believer in the growth of the territory and invested in businesses with that in mind. He produced railroad ties for the Dakota Southern and graded the route for the Northern Pacific into Bismarck.

By the summer of 1873, trains were running into both Yankton and Bismarck, and the two Dakota cities became ports. In both cases, their development as ports was enhanced by the financial Panic of 1873, which led to a worldwide depression. For the railroad industry in the United States, the key event was on September 18, 1873, when Jay Cooke and Company closed its doors and the railroads it financed were part of the cascade effect of economic woes. For Bismarck and Yankton, it meant that railroad construction stopped at their respective sites on the Missouri. Railheads on a

Early Bismarck, after the period of being the "Wickedest City in the West." *Author's collection.*

Fort Abraham Lincoln. *Courtesy Fort Abraham Lincoln Foundation.*

navigable river made natural ports and centers for transshipment, requiring warehouses and workers.

It was also in September 1873 that George Custer arrived at the new cavalry post at Fort Abraham Lincoln. Along with Fort Hancock alongside the Northern Pacific rails in downtown Bismarck, Fort Abraham Lincoln was established in 1872 as a two-company infantry post. It was named at first for Colonel H. Boyd McKeen, who had fallen at the Battle of Cold Harbor. In November 1872, it was renamed for the fallen president, and in March 1873, a cavalry post was authorized by Congress to be built adjacent to the infantry. The Seventh Cavalry met an April blizzard in Yankton and spent the summer protecting Northern Pacific surveyors in Montana, where they fought Sitting Bull, Rain-in-the-Face and Gall for the first time. In September, Custer and his men settled into Fort Lincoln, just southwest across the river from Bismarck. Each site was a frequent stop for steamboats.

Chapter 16

THE *FAR WEST* AND GRANT PRINCE MARSH

Libbie, a drawing of Elizabeth Bacon Custer by Mark Kenneweg. *Courtesy Fort Abraham Lincoln Foundation and the Kenneweg family.*

Elizabeth Bacon Custer—"Libbie" to her devoted husband, George Armstrong Custer—was a force to be reckoned with. She married the youngest general in U.S. history while he was still engaged in the Civil War. She began then her career as a camp follower.

When the postwar army ranged the Plains under Libbie's brevet general, who became first a captain and later a lieutenant colonel, she stayed as close as possible. *Tenting on the Plains* is her story of Lieutenant Colonel Custer in Kansas, but it is also an autobiography. Rare among army wives, Libbie exerted every effort to stand by her man.

On May 17, 1876, Libbie rode with the one-thousand-man caravan out of Fort Abraham Lincoln.

Arikara scouts led the way for two circuits around the fort's parade ground and over the hills west to a campsite on both sides of the Heart River fourteen miles from Fort Lincoln. Libbie spent that first night of the campaign that culminated in the stunning defeat of the Seventh Cavalry next to her husband. It was their last night together.

Libbie, though, had other plans.

Ten days after the soldiers left Fort Lincoln, the *Far West* riverboat steamed up from the south and docked at the fort. Riverboat landings were always a welcome diversion from the daily routines at frontier military posts, and they were especially appreciated by the ladies of the forts. The wives of Fort Lincoln officers crowded on board while the *Far West* unloaded goods and loaded small arms ammunition and other supplies intended for the men marching to Montana.

Captain Grant Marsh ordered as dainty a lunch set for the ladies as his boat could afford. They dined in the long, sky-lit hallway sandwiched between the two rows of cabins on the second deck. Other than Marsh's own spacious cabin, the others were tiny six- by nine-foot sleeping compartments with doors opening to the outside and into the dining hall. That common area was used for meetings, dinners and common space where passengers could while away their time with card games and conversation.

Marsh attempted to personally supervise the unloading and loading, but Mrs. Custer would not hear of it. She insisted that the captain join the ladies for lunch, and he complied, making himself presentable for polite company as quickly as he could. At lunch, Libbie and the wife of Lieutenant Algernon Smith made certain to sit near Marsh and were, in the words of his friend and biographer Joseph Hanson, "at particular pains to treat him cordially."[61] The charming conversation had an ulterior motive, which was revealed as Marsh excused himself to get back to work. The two women drew Marsh aside and pitched their plan. They would like to ride the *Far West* to its meeting with the regiment on the Yellowstone River.

When Marsh was hired for the summer's work by General Phil Sheridan, he was asked to pick the boat he wanted to captain. The two boats he considered were both the latest style of mountain boats. The key changes brought by mountain boats were abandoning side-wheels for a stern paddlewheel, shallow drafts and reduced height profile to minimize the effects of wind on navigation.

Marsh had been captain of the steamer *Josephine*, a good shallow-draft boat with more—and more comfortable—cabin space. Anticipating a long season of tough work, Marsh opted for the *Far West* for two principle reasons. He didn't want the cabin space because he definitely did not want to host

Stereoscopic photo of the interior of the *Far West* cabin deck by F. Jay Haynes. *State Historical Society of North Dakota.*

passengers, and the boat had two capstans instead of one, giving it more flexibility in overcoming sandbars and low-water situations.

The captain discouraged the ladies, pointing out the cabin space, which he considered inadequate for their station as delicate officers' wives. Libbie

George, a drawing of George Armstrong Custer by Mark Kenneweg. *Courtesy Fort Abraham Lincoln Foundation and the Kenneweg family*.

had ridden with Custer's cavalry and shared his tents many times over their thirteen-year marriage. She was not dissuaded easily. The dangers of supposed Indian attacks didn't work either. The debate continued, with Libbie declaring truthfully that her general had authorized the excursion if Captain Marsh would allow it. Marsh finally expressed his regrets that if only he had chosen the *Josephine*, he would have been happy to carry the two passengers. As it was, he was required by circumstances to decline. The captain won the day, but he had to explain his position again when a disappointed George found that his wife was not on board when the *Far West* made its rendezvous with the regiment at the mouth of the Big Horn.

DR. HENRY RENALDO PORTER

Born: February 13, 1848, Lee Center, New York
Died: March 3, 1903, Agra, India

Dr. Henry R. Porter was the son of Dr. Henry Norton Porter and Helen Porter. Upon graduation from Georgetown Medical School in 1872, Porter became a contract surgeon for the army, assigned to the most inaccessible and desolate part of the Republic, Fort Whipple near Prescott, Arizona. After campaigning with General Crook's Fifth Cavalry in desert heat and mountain cold in country Porter believed better left to the Indians, the young surgeon declared himself able to "ride fifty miles or walk fifteen as well as any of the old soldiers."

Dr. Porter's second army contract brought him to Camp Hancock in the growing new city of Bismarck in October 1873. George Custer's Seventh Cavalry had moved into Fort Abraham Lincoln on the other side of the Missouri in just the previous month. On May 17, 1876, when Camp

"Lonesome" Charley Reynolds, famed frontier scout who died at the Battle of the Little Big Horn. *Courtesy Fort Abraham Lincoln Foundation.*

Hancock's Seventeenth Infantry joined Custer in General Alfred Terry's Dakota Column on its way to Montana, Dr. Porter was one of three accompanying physicians. On June 25, the other two would die. Porter survived, to the benefit of dozens of the wounded at the Battle of the Little Big Horn.

With Reno's column when it was flanked and routed, Porter was helping ease the pain of a fatally wounded soldier when he heard Reno shout "Charge!" The charge was a chaotic advance to the rear, retreating across the Little Big Horn and up a steep ravine under heavy attack. To the Indians, the fleeing soldiers were as easy to kill as buffalo. Porter was late to the retreat, leaving his dying patient only upon the urging of famed frontier scout Lonesome Charley Reynolds, who was himself killed moments later. Porter rode well, as he'd bragged, and outrode less fortunate soldiers through the river and up the ravine.

On the bluff, he quickly went to work, treating each wounded man as he found them while the soldiers established a defensive perimeter. An hour after the retreat began, with enemy firing much reduced and Captain Benteen's pack train arrived, a field hospital was established for the thirteen most seriously wounded. The hospital was protected by the pack train's horses, mules, boxes and saddles.

After Custer's battalion had been eliminated, heavy firing resumed and before the very late June sun set, another six wounded entered the field hospital. Porter and two orderlies worked without sufficient water to wash wounds, or clean dressings. In the calm of darkness, Porter could work without fear of snipers, but he couldn't see well enough to be sure he was able to remove foreign matter from wounds. A German private, doomed by a bullet through his intestines, cried for water he couldn't have. He died in

Curly, the young Crow scout who delivered word of the Battle of the Little Big Horn to Grant Marsh. *Courtesy Fort Abraham Lincoln Foundation.*

the night. It was a tough night for the survivors as well. The feelings of panic they'd shared in the chaotic "Charge!" returned with time to ruminate on the overwhelming force that surrounded their weak little fort. With morning, heavy sniper fire began again. It continued heavy into the afternoon, then became more sporadic, intended to keep the soldiers busy as the Indian camp began to move in a scene remembered by one private as a "Biblical exodus; the Israelites moving into Egypt; a mighty tribe on the march."[62]

Reno's beleaguered men were no longer besieged. Water for horses and wounded was obtained. Porter's makeshift field hospital overflowed with fifty-nine wounded. Their real hospital was far away.

The wounded began to be moved from the battlefield late on June 28. Litters made from the hides of downed horses had been constructed to carry those who couldn't ride. Some casualties were carried by teams of four men; others rode between two mules. About thirty hours after they

Drawing of the sternwheel packet *Far West. Courtesy Special Collections, Murphy Library, University of Wisconsin–La Crosse.*

started their journey, Dr. Porter could see a fire-lit path to the more-than-welcome torch-lit *Far West.* There he found that Captain Grant Marsh had prepared for hosting wounded soldiers. The deck was spread with fresh-cut prairie grass and covered with canvas.

Dr. Porter finally had a field hospital worthy of its name. Forty-two wounded men were bedded down, their wounds examined and dressed, and each was offered a well-deserved stiff pull of whiskey.

Captain Marsh's run from the Big Horn to Bismarck, via the Yellowstone and Missouri Rivers, became a legend. It was a fifty-four-hour, 710-mile race day and night with brief stops only for wood and to spread information.

Forty of the wounded were soldiers; two were Arikara scouts. Famed scout Goose left the boat at Fort Berthold. Three soldiers died on the trip. Thirty-eight were admitted to the hospital at Fort Lincoln.

There they immediately got another change of bandages, wound cleaning and, no doubt much to the patients' delight, new underwear. Some surgeries to remove bullets or bits of cloth stuck in wounds had been too dangerous to perform on the move and in the field. The surgeries were finally attended to, two weeks after they were inflicted.

Three days after getting his patients settled, Dr. Porter was on the *Far West* with Grant Marsh again, returning to the Yellowstone River to minister to the soldiers still on campaign. It was an ugly sight he found.

Morale was low, and scurvy was high. Careful and organized, General Terry wouldn't move without proper supply lines. He kept his men in hardtack and bacon, but he overlooked vegetables and vitamin C. Medical supplies of lime juice and pickles were quickly exhausted. The sickest were evacuated by steamboat from the temporary camps along the Yellowstone to Fort Buford and beyond.

Unlike his uncharitable view of Arizona, Porter thought Bismarck had a great future. The town of two thousand at the end of the Northern Pacific line, with its steamboat industry growing, had room for another doctor in private practice. Porter hung out a shingle and continued to serve Camp Hancock on a per-incident basis. He had a contract with the Northern Pacific and later became the county doctor for Burleigh County and the physician for the state penitentiary. He was a founder of the Missouri Valley Medical Society and the Medical Society of North Dakota. He was also a businessman and investor in real estate in Bismarck and the District of Columbia. Porter was a founder of the First National Bank of Bismarck and the State Bank of Morton County.

The war service of Grant Marsh and *Far West* continued, serving Generals Terry and Miles and their dispirited men, helping to move camps, carrying supplies and scouting with a quick strike force.

Miles asked Buffalo Bill Cody to board *Far West* with Louis Richard to scout for Indian trails. Cody wrote, "The idea of scouting on a steamboat was indeed a novel one to me, and I anticipated a pleasant trip."[63]

Cody and Richard were stationed in the pilothouse, each scanning a bank for signs of crossings.

> [The] *steamer, with a full head of steam, went flying past islands, around bends, over sandbars, at a rate that was exhilarating. Presently I thought I could see horses grazing in a distant bend of the river, and I reported the fact to General Miles, who asked Captain Marsh if he could land the boat near a large tree, which he pointed out to him.*
>
> *"Yes, sir; I can land her there, and make her climb the tree if necessary," said he.*
>
> *...While we were getting ashore, Captain Marsh remarked that if there was only a good heavy dew on the grass he would shoot the steamer ashore, and take us on the scout without the trouble of leaving the boat.*[64]

The winter of 1876–77 was a hard one for the free Lakota. "Custer's Avengers" swelled enlistment in the frontier army. Miles pursued and harassed Crazy Horse and Sitting Bull. The latter slipped into Canada with

The *Far West*, loaded. *Courtesy Special Collections, Murphy Library, University of Wisconsin–La Crosse.*

his Hunkpapa. Without ever losing a battle, the Lakota lost the war. Soldiers destroyed camp after camp and forced Crazy Horse to ride into Camp Robinson in a kind of triumphal surrender on May 5, 1877.

With the war over and the region occupied by soldiers, settlers poured into the Yellowstone valley. Although military contracts eventually waned, new settlers meant new commerce, and between 1872 and 1883, steamboats were the most efficient way settlers could get their products to market and get everything to make their new towns grow.

Rails were laid on ice to get a steam engine to the west bank of the Missouri by Bismarck. *Courtesy Fort Abraham Lincoln Foundation.*

Adjacent to Fort Keogh in 1878, the port at Miles City saw a couple dozen steamboats land. In 1880, the Yellowstone valley population was 1,300 and growing. Fort Keogh drew government contracts. Grant Marsh owned their business, but trains were on their way. Track was laid west of the Missouri before a bridge reached the west bank. An engine crossed the river on tracks laid on winter ice, a scene commemorated by a contemporary *Harpers* magazine engraving. Supplies were ferried across and the engine relayed them to the end of the track.

GRANT PRINCE MARSH

Born: May 11, 1834, Rochester, Pennsylvania
Died: January 2, 1916, Bismarck, North Dakota

Marsh lived in Yankton but made his living almost entirely between the port of Bismarck and the growing Yellowstone valley. He piloted the *F.Y. Batchelor* to Fort Buford with the last cargo of a lengthy navigable season on November 4, 1880. Marsh's plans of immediately returning the boat to Bismarck and himself to his wife in Yankton for the winter were interrupted by the officer of commissary at the fort. Captain Woodruff explained to Marsh that a post 318 miles away was in need. Where the Musselshell River enters the Missouri, a small detachment of soldiers prepared to winter in a place vulnerable to hit-and-run attacks from Sitting Bull's people in Canada. Unbeknownst to those at Buford, the twenty-one soldiers and scouts at the post on the Musselshell were attacked by a large party of Lakota on November 6, lending urgency to Woodruff's concern for their survival.

Captain Grant Prince Marsh. *State Historical Society of North Dakota.*

Woodruff asked Marsh to extend his season with a run to the Musselshell. Considering the various uncertain risks, particularly low and soon-to-be-frozen water, Marsh wasn't eager to go, but his standing with the army wasn't based on avoiding difficult assignments. The *Batchelor* would take the task for $350 per day. Captain Woodruff pointed out that the *General Terry*, similar to the *F.Y. Batchelor* in all respects other than its chief officer, was also docked at Buford. The *General Terry*'s pilot, Captain Sims, offered to take on the mission for $160 per day. Marsh wouldn't relent on his rate. Woodruff wanted Marsh but wouldn't make the decision to spend nearly double the low rate without orders from headquarters. Woodruff telegraphed the human General Terry for advice. Terry authorized the spending to get Marsh, and the mission was launched. Oats and other supplies were loaded, and a detachment of Seventh Infantry came aboard. The water was low and the steamboat needed to be worked over difficult passages, but the *Batchelor* still made good time and by late morning on November 12 got to the Musselshell, where its

The *F.Y. Batchelor* tied up to shore. *Author's collection.*

supplies and soldiers were unloaded quickly. Marsh got under way downriver that afternoon, but it was too late. The *Batchelor* was stuck in ice near the Milk River. Marsh left a crew to tend to the boat and made his way back to Yankton by way of wagon. It was a very cold trip, and he feared for frostbite but made it home intact.

The following spring found Marsh on his way back to the boat. Instead of the first boat of the 1881 navigation season coming from Yankton or Bismarck, it came from upriver. Marsh's men extricated the *Batchelor* and headed for Fort Union. Gathering up a cargo of $106,000 worth of hides and furs, Marsh got a jump on one of the last great years of the fur trade.

As the end of the Minnesota Uprising led to steamboats transporting Indians as actual or virtual prisoners, so did the end of the ill-fated campaign of 1876–77. After cashing in on *F.Y. Batchelor*'s early start, for the rest of 1881, Marsh captained the *Eclipse*, one of four boats assigned to bring three thousand Sioux from Fort Keogh by Miles City in Montana Territory to Fort Randall in the southern half of Dakota.

Sitting Bull, *Tatanka Iyatake*, Hunkpapa spiritual and strategic leader. *Courtesy Fort Abraham Lincoln Foundation.*

The next year, Marsh met Sitting Bull. After his 1881 surrender at the Fort Buford he had attacked a decade and a half before, Sitting Bull was taken to Fort Randall as a prisoner. In 1882, Grant Marsh and the packet *W.J. Behan* were assigned to move the Hunkpapa leader, his two wives and his children—altogether 170 of his people—to their new home on the Standing Rock Sioux Reservation at Fort Yates.

During the voyage, Sitting Bull was a great celebrity. Marsh said that his passenger had been taught in Canada to write his name in English. This would be in addition to the way he already knew, which was a drawing of a sitting bull buffalo. He also knew the value of money and accepted payment of a dollar for every autograph he graciously signed for the Dakotans crowding the banks at each stop for *W.J. Behan*.

At the Cheyenne River Agency, Marsh, somewhat of a hero to the frontier military, was presented with a lovely pipestem. Marsh showed it to Sitting Bull, who was impressed enough to offer to buy it. Marsh didn't want to sell it, but as Sitting Bull pursued the matter, Marsh set the price at fifty dollars. Sitting Bull was indignant. Fifty dollars was too much.

Marsh might have thought he was funny when he said to the interpreter, "Well, tell him he has kept me scared for twenty years along the river and he ought to give me something for that."

"I did not come on your land to scare you," Sitting Bull pointed out. "If you had not come on my land, you would not have been scared, either."[65]

Marsh got the point. Sitting Bull did not get the pipe.

Chapter 17

BISMARCK'S VICTORY

As the years of hot military action morphed into occupation duty, the writing was on the wall for steamboat commerce on the upper Missouri. The days of regular epic voyages from St. Louis to Fort Benton were over. Bismarck and Yankton remained commercial ports for shipping as convenient to rail heads. The financial Panic of 1873 temporarily stopped westward expansion of rails for Yankton as well as Bismarck. In Bismarck, the lack of a Missouri River bridge was the impediment. In Yankton, it was the lack of federal subsidization of the construction.

That situation could not and did not last. Railroads extended to the Missouri upstream from Yankton, and as Joseph Mills Hanson wrote, "Though Yankton had not totally lost her river trade in 1878, 1879, and 1880, it was on the wane, and Bismarck built up by the Northern Pacific Railroad, was profiting by the older city's loss."

Bismarck thrived.

In a front-page editorial on September 5, 1877, the *Bismarck Tri-Weekly Tribune* called for a Marine Hospital to be built in Bismarck. Its justification was Bismarck's suddenly preeminent position as a Missouri River port.

"It is conceded by the best informed steamboat men that more boating has been done between Bismarck and the military posts up the Missouri this season than anywhere else in the whole country," the *Tribune* stated. It noted that despite 1,200 steamboat men on the upper river paying $0.40 a month to support treatment for those injured in steamboat accidents (in a typical six-month season an amount totaling $2,880), there was virtually

Eclipse (foreground) at Port of Bismarck in 1880. Other steamboats include *Red Cloud*, *Nellie Peck* and *Gen. Tompkins*. *Courtesy Special Collections, Murphy Library, University of Wisconsin–La Crosse.*

no chance it would be used by those in Bismarck and beyond. There was no marine hospital closer than St. Louis or Galena, and with traffic on the lower river so irregular, an injured steamboat man would have to pay $50 in rail passenger charges to get to a hospital. And, the article added, "a sick man might die long before he could reach there."

The editorial noted that as lower river traffic had become "irregular," it had been supplanted. "The navigable waters of the upper Missouri and Yellowstone will be the fields for successful steamboat enterprise." There were thirty-seven boats operating above Bismarck in 1877, according to the newspaper.

The *Tribune* sold lots of advertising related to steamboats, even for those on the Red River. The Northern Pacific promoted service to Fort Garry. Its rails reached Fargo, and steamboats would take it from there. The paper also reported the status of the steamboats. On September 5, 1877, *Far West* was on its way to Yankton while the *Big Horn*, *Josephine*, *Benton*, *Custer*, *Mead* and *Peninah* were all at the landing.

On November 4, 1878, the *Tribune* reported that James A. Emmons, head of the Marine Ways and Dock Company, was building a new dock and ways to dock six steamboats. His business would extend beyond repairing steamboats to include building them. To Emmons, Bismarck was a hub city of a prosperous and growing region: "Dakota and Montana mountains are chock full of gold, silver, copper, tin and coal. That country is the Ophir of America as far as valuable minerals are concerned." He had plans to expand the ways to cover six hundred feet of riverfront. His shipyard would get its timber from the oak and pine along the Northern Pacific rail line, and it would bring its boilers and engines from the east by rail, as well. The finished product would save the costs of a long boat trip from Pittsburgh.

> *It means millions though to our town, the Northern Pacific and our steamboat lines. The Steamer Mcleod has just arrived from Benton leaving there in the middle of October. The McCleod, Benton, and Key West will repair on our ways and be ready to leave for the golden mountains forty days earlier in the spring than ever before....*
>
> *Bismarck in the next twenty years will become the largest town on the Missouri. No other city on the river has the natural advantages that Bismarck has. Her river front will soon be lined with stockyards, ship yards, foundries, saw mills, smelting works and grain elevators. The opening up of the Upper Missouri River country and the Yellowstone region make all these things necessary.*[66]

Emmons, though he ended up with a North Dakota county named after him, was more booster than prophet.

Bismarck's port status faced a threat.

Chapter 18

THE NORTHERN PACIFIC CROSSES THE MISSOURI

The paralysis that struck rail construction with the Panic of 1873 did not last long in the expanding United States. The Crossing would finally get its bridge.

George Morison was tagged to engineer the job. Detroit Bridge & Iron Works was hired to build it. While the river was only wide, its sandy bottom was soft and deep. Making proper supports for the bridge solid would require some work. Second, the profile of the bridge needed to accommodate the smokestacks of steamboats. During high-water incidents lower on the river, railroad bridges had prevented passage by steamboats or, in at least one case, had required sawing off some smokestack.

Morison designed the bridge to work, to last and to not interfere with steamboat traffic. It provided seventy feet of clearance above the normal level of the Missouri. It was built in sections and laid across substantial caissons sunk deep through the millennia of sand deposits into more solid earth.

As the Northern Pacific had continued laying track on the west side of the Missouri before the bridge was built, within months of the bridge's completion, the railroad had reached Glendive, connecting the Yellowstone valley with the world in a new, faster and safer way.

Instantly, Bismarck's realm shrunk. Its steamboat industry was diminished. However, at the same time, its leadership position in Dakota Territory was being solidified by political action led by the self-interest of the Northern Pacific.

In 1883, Yankton lost another significant competition with Bismarck. The city on the Northern Pacific Line became territorial capital in 1883.

The railroad bridge across the Missouri at Bismarck. *Author's collection.*

The whole process shows much about the role of government in the era of robber barons, and the role of robber barons in government.

Alexander McKenzie had thrived in Bismarck's bloody years. He was sheriff for a time and an early business leader. He invested in a water company, which became the city's source of residential and business water, as well as water for the railroad. By 1882, he was a significant figure in Republican politics in the territory and a slick lobbyist for the Northern Pacific. In the 1883 session of the territorial legislature, McKenzie put in motion a deep plan with a lot of moving parts. First, McKenzie's aides began agitating to move the capital to Huron or another town more central to the territory. Second, they convinced the legislature to establish a commission to study the subject, and granted it the extraordinary authority to pick the capital. Territorial governor Nehemiah G. Ordway, a good friend of the Northern Pacific and a McKenzie ally, got to name the ten commissioners. McKenzie was named one of them. He became chairman of the relocation executive committee.

A quirk in the act establishing the commission was the requirement that the first meeting of the commission be held in Yankton. Knowing the local mood toward losing the capital and fearing local law enforcement could carry injunctions or writs, McKenzie came up with a solution. He brought the commissioners to Sioux City, where they boarded a Milwaukee Road train at 3:00 a.m. and set out for Yankton. McKenzie aides had marked the extreme legal limits of Yankton along the tracks so the car carrying the commission

Pierre's first resident steamboat was a ferry named *Jim Leighton*, which began service in 1880, according to William Lass. *Courtesy Special Collections, Murphy Library, University of Wisconsin–La Crosse.*

could slow within the city boundary. At 5:15 a.m., the commission was called to order. With the train still rolling slowly, commission members elected a president, set a date for their next meeting in Canton and adjourned. An angry crowd of deputy sheriffs and others waving writs watched as the train pulled through the station without stopping.

Many towns wanted the capital. Aberdeen, Bismarck, Canton, Frankfort, Huron, Mitchell, Odessa, Ordway, Pierre, Redfield and Steele all submitted bids. To improve Bismarck's bid, the Northern Pacific donated 160 acres for the capitol. McKenzie sweetened the reception the final choice would have by giving $10,000 checks to each of ten legislators. After visiting each of the towns, or proposed town sites, the commission met in Fargo to pick a town. McKenzie put on a virtuoso performance, biding his time, voting for Steele on a second ballot and then shepherding Bismarck's vote total from one, to zero, to one and then steadily gaining support through thirteen ballots. Bismarck became the capital.

At statehood, November 2, 1889, South Dakota chose centrally located Pierre as its capital. Yankton has yet to regain its status. Bismarck remained the capital of the state drawn from the northern half of the territory.

Chapter 19

THE LAST DAYS OF DAKOTA STEAMBOATS

In the 1880s, steamboat business on the Missouri became confined to ferries and local work in between rail lines out of Yankton and Running Water in the southern half of Dakota and the portion between Bismarck and Fort Benton. The leading figure in the latter business was Isaac Post Baker.

Northern Pacific on George Morison's bridge between Bismarck and Mandan. *Courtesy Fort Abraham Lincoln Foundation.*

ISAAC P. BAKER

Born: July 20, 1855, Weston, Missouri
Died: January 28, 1938, Bismarck, North Dakota

Isaac P. Baker was born into the riverboat business. After attending Central College at Fayette, Missouri, Baker went to work with his father, John Baker, in management of the St. Paul and St. Louis Packet Company. His uncle Isaac G. Baker was Pierre Chouteau Jr.'s last agent in Fort Benton. Uncle I.G. stayed at Fort Benton after Chouteau sold out and operated a general merchandise business there at the terminus of Missouri navigation.

In 1880, Isaac P. went to work for Thomas C. Power as general agent for the Benton Transportation Company, assigned to run operations in Bismarck. To say I.P. was a confident and headstrong young man might be an understatement. Power that year entered into an anti-competition pool arrangement with the Peck Line. Both companies ran steamboats into Fort Benton from Dakota. In 1881, the remaining competitor for that trade, the Coulson Line, also joined the pool. Recognizing Baker's skills in implementing an efficient means of bookkeeping, requisitioning and budgeting, the group named I.P. as their pool agent. He was efficient, but he was also smart, ruthless and loyal only to Power and himself.

Baker incensed Power's partners by making a separate deal to also serve as agent for the I.G. Baker Company and shipping some of the pool's freight on his uncle's steamboat *Red Cloud*. Coulson and Peck demanded a meeting to discuss it. Baker attended but stormed out of the August 1881 meeting, declaring over his retreating shoulder that he "decline[d] to have anything more to do with the pool," while proclaiming his loyalty to Power's interests. The end of the pool was in sight.[67]

The Peck Line had more problems than solutions, and one of those solutions might indicate why the line was in trouble.

The Peck Line's *Peninah* was seized on order of the Montana U.S. marshal on allegations that its crew sold alcohol to reservation Indians. It was held under guard at Rock Haven, near Bismarck, where the government intended to winter it while the case moved its way through federal court. Unlike earlier incidents when local sheriffs tried to seize steamboats, like the Johnson boats for the Yellowstone expedition of 1819, simply moving the boat to another county was not going to work against the reach of the government of the United States, but *Peninah*'s captain, David Campbell, didn't seem to know that.

In September 1882, Campbell organized his crew to retake the *Peninah*. Let that sink in. Campbell intended to grab his boat from federal custody and take it—where?

The plan, such as it was, involved classic western fare. Campbell's minions brought a bottle of liquor to Rock Haven and shared it with *Peninah*'s lone guard. While the guard was distracted, Campbell and several crew members snuck on board, got up steam, released the ropes and headed downstream. Other conspirators cut the telegraph lines between Fort Abraham Lincoln and Fort Yates, and the escape, against all odds, seemed to work. But the boat had only one direction in which to flee, and it was in no way going to leave the jurisdiction of the United States.

The telegraph line was repaired. The federal deputy marshal at Pierre was alerted, and *Peninah* was stopped and retaken by the United States.[68]

Despite *Peninah* being on the bench in 1882, the Peck Line had three steamboats—*Far West*, *General Meade* and *General Terry*—operating out of Bismarck that year. The following year, it had only the *General Terry* in service in Dakota Territory. The Peck Line gave up and went out of business before the 1884 navigation season opened. The Coulson Line followed the Peck Line into dissolution a year later, and Baker and the Power line then had a monopoly on steamboat services on the upper Missouri. It would not be a tremendously profitable monopoly. The end was near.

In 1885, Joseph La Barge's brother John dropped dead at the wheel of a steamboat he was docking in Bismarck. The same year, Joseph retired from piloting steamboats. The La Barge story was over, and according to H.M. Chittenden, the entire upper Missouri business was over shortly thereafter. "The final blow," he wrote, "was delivered to the river trade in 1887, when the Great Northern [railroad] reached Helena."

But Isaac P. Baker and Grant Marsh still had some chapters to write.

Marsh retired from upper Missouri work right after delivering Sitting Bull to Fort Yates in 1882. He sold the steamboat *W.J. Behan* in Bismarck, closed his home in Yankton and moved to Memphis, where he ran a ferry on the Mississippi. For two decades, he worked the Mississippi, but in 1903, Marsh received an entreaty from former general W.D. Washburn to come back to Dakota. Washburn was also a former U.S. senator but an active entrepreneur. He bought 115,000 acres of excellent agricultural land a bit north of Bismarck and ran a railroad line to a prospective port on the Missouri. The port would ship out locally found lignite coal and grain produced by Washburn's workers and neighbors. The town that grew around the river port was named, naturally enough, Washburn. The general wrote

The landing at Washburn, North Dakota. *Courtesy Special Collections, Murphy Library, University of Wisconsin–La Crosse.*

to Grant Marsh with a job offer to work his line of small steamboats. Marsh returned to Dakota.

Washburn had a big idea and got something big started, but he preferred not to actually operate a railroad and a steamboat line. His boats ended up owned by I.P. Baker. In 1905, in the pilothouse of the *Weston*, Marsh rescued the Bismarck water system. The river intake for Bismarck was not far south of the railroad bridge. In one of the innumerable shifts the Missouri has made over time, it very quickly created a sandbar that plugged the water intake. Citizens were dry, but perhaps more importantly to the principals involved, so was the railroad. The Northern Pacific happened to have a bridge remodeling crew handy and the engineer in charge of the project had an idea that a steamboat might be put to good use to save the situation. He asked I.P. Baker to name his best pilot. It was Marsh. I.P. and the N.P. put the proposal to Marsh, and he accepted with a concern and a caveat. "I never tried to run a steamboat through a 200-foot sandbar before, but I'll do my best if you will be responsible in case the boat is damaged or lost."[69]

Marsh's biographer Joseph Mills Hanson describes the scene:

> *The next day was Sunday. At eleven o'clock in the morning, Captain Marsh backed the* Weston *down on the head of the bar, close in by the main bank, with her stern wheel resting against the sand. From the bow capstans he ran two long hawsers back past the stern, one on either side of the boat, and fastened the end of each to a large log, or "dead man," buried some distance out on the bar. Then he started the wheel, which, as it revolved, dug out the sand and pushed it toward the bow, with the capstans slowly wound up the hawsers, keeping them taut and pulling the boat back as the wheel cut into the bar. No current from the river, only slack water, followed the boat into the pocket she was making and presently the sand which was being thrown toward the bow began to settle in front of her, leaving her isolated in a small pool. It began to look as though she were going to imprison herself effectually in the heart of the bar, but her captain kept on with his work doggedly.*
>
> *Back on the bluffs, nearly the entire population of Bismarck had assembled to watch the interesting experiment, though not until afterward did the captain know how many intent observers he had on that Sabbath afternoon. Mr. Nickerson* [the NP engineer] *had suspended operations on the bridge and put his entire force to work carrying coal to the* Weston *to keep her boilers going.*
>
> *By mid-afternoon the boat had eaten half way through the bar and it became evident that, unless an accident occurred, her effort was going to be successful. Fortunately, all went well and at half-past nine that night the pounding wheel broke through the last ridge of sand, and the steamer backed triumphantly out into the main channel. Once the way was cleared, the river current surged into the passage and by the following morning the bar had entirely disappeared, the intake pipe was clear and the water famine ended.*

Shortly after restoring water to Bismarck, Marsh was contracted to inspect his old Yellowstone River for the federal government. They wanted his opinion on the practicality of steaming construction materials to a low-head reclamation dam they intended to construct downriver from Glendive. His report was favorable, and the next year, Marsh found himself delivering cement on a forty-mile round trip from Glendive to the dam site on I.P. Baker's steamboat *Expansion.* Baker complained that the dam would completely end Yellowstone River shipping, but he clearly intended to squeeze what profit he could from the dying business model. It was what Baker had been doing for many years.

In 1896, Baker gave up on routes going to Pierre, confining the majority of his business to the region from Fort Yates to Fort Berthold, though he sometimes traveled up the Yellowstone. He continued to operate boats for another twenty-four years, finding efficiencies and niches with smaller gas-powered boats that served river communities lacking rail service.

As Baker had been efficiently operating a declining business, he had been diversifying. Baker and Thomas Power bought the Bank of Bismarck. Baker started the Cannonball Cattle Company, Bismarck Realty Company, Bismarck Elevator and Investment Company and Montana Elevator Company, and he owned elevators at Washburn, Manhaven, Sanger and Deapolis, all north of Bismarck. The *Bismarck Tribune* said in 1938 that Baker "farmed until very recent years as many acres as any man in this section and raised pure bred hogs."

To some degree, Baker succeeded Boss Alexander McKenzie as the biggest kind of big shot in Bismarck, though in a much kinder and gentler way. He was elected to a one-year term as mayor of Bismarck in April 1890, gaining a 160-vote margin on the Democratic ticket. He served on the Democratic National Committee and was a delegate to the Democratic National Convention in Kansas City in 1900 that nominated prairie populist William Jennings Bryan of Nebraska and his running mate Adlai E. Stevenson of Illinois. That happened to be the first major party convention with a female delegate, Elizabeth Cohen of Salt Lake City.

A Bismarck booster, Baker chaired a citizens' committee that successfully advocated for moving the troops stationed at Fort Yates into a new Fort Lincoln, built on the Bismarck side of the river. He was president of the 1915 North Dakota Ag Expo and served as federal fuel administrator for North Dakota during World War I.

Baker told a story about saving a U.S. deputy marshal and sixteen of his deputies from drowning at the hands of striking rail workers in Mandan in 1894. Somehow, the marshal called Baker on the phone at his office. The marshal was in a panic. He said his men were being pursued by two to three thousand "Debs strikers," so called for Eugene Debs, the leader of the rail workers' union. The strikers were pushing his marshals toward the river. "Captain Baker, for God's sake, what am I going to do?"

Baker, coincidentally, had a boat crewed and at the ready. The marshal's call had come almost immediately after Baker put down the telephone informing him of the docking of *F.Y. Batchelor* at the Port of Bismarck. He told the marshal, "Let the mob chase you into the river. Don't shoot, but keep on the road to the river and when you get to the river the steamboat *F.Y. Batchelor* will be at the landing and take you and your men down the river until you meet the troops from Fort Yates." He reiterated, "Don't shoot into the mob."[70]

Baker grabbed the phone again, called the port and ordered the boat into action. Men with Winchesters would line the rail, and boarding planks would be put out to the dock. Baker told his men the same thing he'd said to the marshal: "Don't shoot into the mob."

It worked as Baker had envisioned. No one shot into the mob.

Grant Marsh rode on the last steamboat leaving Fort Benton. It was a government boat, the *Mandan*, doing investigation of the upper river in 1908. Marsh waited for it and joined the boat for the trip downriver, scouting, he told a reporter, for the possibility of I.P. Baker running boats to the Milk River in Montana. Marsh was riding, not captaining. He had lost his license the year before.

In August 1907, Marsh had a dispute with another pilot working for Baker. Marsh went aboard his former boat *Expansion* and got into a confrontation with William Massie. Charges were filed, and on December 8, the Department of Commerce and Labor revoked Marsh's license.

Grant Marsh died in Bismarck in 1916 at age eighty-three. He asked to be buried on Wagon Wheel Bluff, where fifty-two years before he had first set foot in what would become Bismarck. He was not. But he was buried high in Bismarck's St. Mary's Cemetery, where, if you can't quite see the river, you can see where it is.

I.P. Baker sold his last steamboat, *Scarab*, in 1920, the same year that construction began on a bridge between Bismarck and Mandan for automobile and pedestrian traffic. The two events may have been coincidental, but six years later, in 1926, the Liberty Memorial Bridge was a named party in a lawsuit brought by Baker against the State of North Dakota. Baker contended that the bridge had changed the river's current and that its exposed bridge pilings prevented his boats from accessing customers and clients south of the bridge. He asked for $3,800 in damages. The suit went nowhere. North Dakota, at the time, had sovereign immunity, a legal standing that meant that the state had to grant citizens the right to sue the state. The state declined to grant that right.

In his stately home, built for him in 1912 by John Larson, elevated from and closer to the Missouri than downtown Bismarck, I.P. Baker fell and broke his hip on November 17, 1937. He did not recover and ten weeks later died at St. Alexius Hospital.

The *Bismarck Tribune*'s front-page lede for Friday, January 28, 1938, read, "Death has snapped Bismarck's last link with the glamorous days of steamboating on the Missouri and Mississippi rivers. As calmly as the great rivers flow in their broad stretches, life ebbed away from Captain Isaac Post Baker." The paper called him a "staunch old riverman, whose erect carriage and regal bearing marks him apart on the streets of Bismarck."

Baker was succeeded by Julia, his wife of forty-nine years, whom he met in Bismarck. A daughter, also named Julia, remained in Bismarck, married to Willard A. Leach. It was a steamboat marriage. Captain Bill Leach, like so many before him, was involved in the steamboat business from birth. His father, Joseph Sr., operated a company out of the Port of Running Water, the only point between Yankton and Chamberlain where a railroad touched the Missouri. Willard was secretary for the company. So the owner of the Fort Benton Packet Company married his daughter off to the son of the owner of the Missouri River Company. It was a merger of two companies and the two Dakotas, but it was a politically mixed marriage. While I.P. was a sturdy Democrat, Joseph Sr. was an uncompromising Republican member of the South Dakota legislature.

Another thing Leach and Baker shared was ownership of *F.Y. Batchelor*. Baker had used *Batchelor* to rescue the marshal from the Debs strikers. Joseph Leach bought the boat after the navigation season in 1906. It had quite a history. Grant Marsh used it to set a Bismarck–Fort Benton speed record in 1878. Then it struck rocks and sunk in lower Dakota. It was raised and put back into service for nearly three decades more. In 1890, *F.Y. Batchelor* delivered the last commercial shipment of goods by riverboat to Fort Benton. The boat had proven very useful for I.P Baker, but Leach's purchase of the boat had unfortunate timing. He was unable to ever operate it. *F.Y. Batchelor* was wrecked by ice near Running Water in March 1907.

On Devils Lake, in north-central North Dakota, a different kind of steamboat ran. The *Minnie H.* was the product of entrepreneur Edward Heerman, who struggled against a rugged winter of 1882 to build the steamboat on the east shore of the big lake, in one of its extensive periods. It was a big boat and a lake boat. Its hull was V-shaped, unlike the flatter-bottomed boats on the Missouri. It carried 150 tons and was 110.0 feet long and 20.0 feet wide. It drew 3.5 feet. Launched in 1883, *Minnie H.* carried mail, passengers and freight on a daily schedule to Fort Totten, at the time both a military post and Sioux reservation, and three times a week to Minnewauken. Lake levels dropped over the next two decades, and towns that had been lakeside became landlocked. *Minnie H.* went out of business in 1906.[71]

North Dakota's preeminent historian Elwyn Robinson's fifth of six themes in his *History of North Dakota* is the Too Much Mistake, the idea that

Minnie H., the deep-hulled lake boat that steamed Devils Lake, 1883–1906. *State Historical Society of North Dakota.*

boosters and optimism about unrealistic growth projections created a state with too many towns, too many banks, too many farms and more.[72] The Too Much Mistake merged with the Saber-Toothed Tiger Curriculum (STC) in the Fairview Lift Bridge over the Yellowstone near its confluence with the Missouri. The STC derives from the joke about the first man who learned to kill the saber-tooths. He taught it to everyone. Soon the dangerous saber-tooth was extinct. Five thousand years later, the Saber-Toothed Tiger Curriculum was still being taught. It was a classical education.

In a postscript to the end of steamboating in Dakota, a bridge over the Yellowstone was erected in 1913. The Fairview Lift Bridge, a quarter-mile-long span at what is locally called the Big Opening, is two miles east of East Fairview, North Dakota on the border with Fairview, Montana. It was part of an aborted attempt by the Great Northern Railroad to stimulate and capture growth in commerce in east-central Montana.

Government regulation of bridges, which had been slow to come in the first place, was now slow to recognize the end of an era. The Yellowstone and Missouri were considered navigable streams, so federal regulations obtained. Bridges over navigable streams needed to accommodate steamboats that would never run again. The Fairview Lift Bridge met the 80-foot height requirement by a counterweight system in two 108-foot-high towers that would lift a 300-foot section of the bridge when needed. It tested perfectly upon completion, lifting the seven-hundred-ton bridge section for the first time. It was also the only time. For nearly half a century, the bridge served railroads and autos, cars passing over on planks laid between and around the tracks. The river it crosses no longer hears the whistle of steamboats. Paddlefish, not paddlewheels, fill the Yellowstone today.

EPILOGUE

Throughout the history of the march of Europeans and their descendants crowding out and forcibly replacing Native Americans across the continent, there was a recurring conflict between those non-Indians who understood and appreciated Indian culture and those who didn't understand or didn't care. Summing up the actual and alternative histories of the intercontinental relations, Hiram Chittenden, writing at the beginning of the twentieth century, reflected the view of the conquering invaders that there was only one possible outcome, and that was total occupation of the continent by people originally from Europe. "It was the decree of destiny that the European should displace the native American upon his own soil. No earthly power could prevent it." He recognized this as a moral wrong and as presenting a conundrum, "how to deprive the Indian of his birthright in such a way that he should feel that no injustice had been done him."[73]

Chittenden thought the kindest route might have been to deny Indian sovereignty and conduct a declared war of conquest rather than forging treaties the United States never intended to keep. "It was throughout a policy of insincerity; the fostering of a spirit of independent sovereignty when in fact the tribes were only vassals."

Hindsight is not always twenty-twenty. Alternatives never taken are not subject to certain projection. History is not predetermined. But even if it were, the persons living it seldom know its determination. There were individuals making decisions, arguing for policies and contending with their present who represented alternative views.

Within his unyielding justification of Manifest Destiny, Chittenden made a very important observation about the march of history in regard to relations between the nations. Noting that the first Euro-American visitors were welcomed to the lodges of the natives, he drew a line between trade and occupation:

> *Under the fur-trade regime the Indian might have continued his native mode of life indefinitely. The trader never sought to change it. He introduced but few innovations; had no desire to introduce any; and looked with as jealous an eye as the Indian himself upon the approach of civilization. This relation of the two races was ideal, and during its continuance the Indian is seen at his best. All this was changed when the emigrant came.... The emigrants came by the thousand and spread themselves all over the country....Before this ever-increasing host the game wasted away. It was estimated that in the single year 1853 four hundred thousand buffalo were slain....Its extermination meant inevitable starvation or hopeless dependence upon the government.*

The devil is always in the details. Overlooked in the rosy view of the fur-trade regime was the conflict created by trappers, who were not exactly agents of civilization and overcrowding but were perceived accurately by the Indians as competition. The battles over trapping predated and preceded steamboat operations in Dakota and Montana. The fur-trade regime's most peaceful era of coexistence lay on top of a successful intrusion of professional trappers competing commercially with the Indians while rapidly depleting the resource from which they profited.

The conflict that would arise from allowing trappers to invade Indian lands was predictable and predicted. It was against the law. Official United States policy in the first decades after independence was to avoid conflict with its neighbors, but after the War of 1812, expansion of the fur trade and border security in the West became policy as well. To the traders in St. Louis, trapping was a logical extension of their business, and while official federal policy didn't quickly change, they took the liberalization of licensing to be a yellow, if not a green, light to flood the upper Missouri and Yellowstone Rivers and the Rockies with company men loaded with traps.

When the fur trade became the robe trade, Plains Indians regained premier position as producers. With their centuries-old experience in hunting buffalo and processing meat and hides, plus the available person-power to hunt and skin, they could dominate the robe trade while feeding their families. Trappers competed more successfully for the less abundant furs that were worth more per pound. They all came together, the trappers and the buffalo hunters, at Fort Union and other trading posts, in a rendezvous culture linked to global commerce by steamboats.

The steamboats brought welcome goods to the Indian nations and then brought an epidemic of unimaginable proportions, followed by soldiers. The technology participated in and facilitated the transformation of the northern plains. It hurried that transformation by several decades. It didn't cause the change.

Indian leaders like Sitting Bull and Gall opposed the steamboats for good reason. They were an effective weapon of war for the Americans. They also brought miners and created settlements, crowding the original inhabitants. The steamboat *St. Peters* carried a cargo of death to the Mandan, Hidatsa, Arikara and Assiniboine. Even at its most benign, the era of steamboats had a tremendous effect on the nature of the upper Missouri. They ate wood ravenously.

In the centuries before 1500, Mandan villages existed for only thirty-five to fifty years, presumably because of an exhaustion of the local wood resource. Their early earthlodges had been rectangular, often with two fire pits and smoke holes. They used a lot of wood. Adoption of construction techniques resulting in round lodges saved trees. Villages became permanent. They lasted centuries, failing only after the devastation of smallpox.

The riverbank forests attracted bison seeking shelter near the earthlodge villages. As the steamboats' hunger stripped the valley of its trees, the bison found other places to seek shelter, compounding problems for the Mandan, Hidatsa and Arikara. If they couldn't call the bison close to their villages, they needed to seek them farther afield, where conflict with Lakota and Dakota people was likely.

For the non-Indians involved with steamboats, they provided relatively rapid and generally safe transportation, commerce and communication. Steamboats stimulated the growth of cities, and as settlements increased in number and size, the boats stitched the region together, serving a local commerce that had grown up after the global commerce they had facilitated in the 1830s and 1840s. They continued serving rural riverside communities until the age of automobiles. The steamboat era also created a legendary cast of characters and a riverside view of historical events in which they played an important role. For the twenty-first-century reader, most of all what steamboats provided were stories. Some of the stories involved a peaceful meeting of cultures while others recounted a clash of cultures, and many were filled with colorful individuals—pilots, entrepreneurs and chiefs.

For those who care about history, the stories of the steamboat era do one very important thing. They layer our past with complexity. The overriding story of exploitation, conquest and relocation has periods of friendships, marriages and mutually profitable commerce interspersing those of military conflict and the confinement of the last free bands of northern Plains Indians.

George Santayana famously said that those who don't remember history are condemned to repeat it. He was wrong. Steamboats won't conduct the fur trade on the Missouri again, whether we remember it or not. History is neither cyclical nor linear, at least not in a predestined or directed way. Voltaire called it a pack of tricks we play on the dead. Napoleon said it was written by the winners. Churchill was sure it would be kind to him because he intended to write it. What history really provides is instruction on human nature and object lessons on ways people interact and organize their societies. The era of the steamboat in Dakota Territory coincided with great changes in the relations between the cultures of the first people of the region and invaders from the United States. The story of the steamboats and the men of the steamboats is a lens through which we see the struggle that the first people faced and the effect of the inexorable occupation of the region by the invaders. We see the Indian villages reduced in number and the pioneer towns of Dakota develop. The men who rode and piloted the steamboats chronicled all those changes. They told the stories.

NOTES

Introduction

1. GreatRiverRoad.com, "Visitor's Guide."

Chapter 1

2. Chardon, *Chardon's Journal*, 63.

Chapter 2

3. Albert Richardson, quoted in *Rivermen*, 7.
4. Potter, *Sheheke*, 79.

Chapter 3

5. Wischmann, *Frontier Diplomats*, 225.
6. Jenkinson, *Vast and Open Plain*.
7. Jackson, *Letters of the Lewis and Clark Expedition*, 435.
8. Douglas, *Manuel Lisa*.
9. Ibid., 88.

10. Ibid., 88–89.
11. Ibid., 88.
12. Bates letter to George Rogers Clark, December 1897, 153.
13. Luttig, *Journal of a Fur-Trading Expedition*, 82–83.
14. Potter, *Sheheke*, 180

Chapter 4

15. Wikipedia footnote to Aeliopile, "De Architectura."
16. Ibid., "Section 50: The Steam Engine."
17. Hunter, *Steamboats on the Western Rivers.*

Chapter 5

18. Lass, *Navigating the Missouri*, 36–38.
19. Ibid., 54–57.

Chapter 6

20. Nester, *Arikara War*, 121.
21. Ibid., 118.
22. Ibid., from Daniel T. Potts journal, 122.
23. Ibid., 141–43.
24. Fenn, *Encounters at the Heart of the World*, 282–83.

Chapter 7

25. Atkinson, *Wheel Boats on the Missouri*, quoting *Edwardsville Spectator*, July 3, 1819, 199.
26. Kappler, *Indian Affairs*, 237.
27. Jensen, and Hutchins, *Wheel Boats on the Missouri*, 209.
28. Kappler, *Indian Affairs*, 227.
29. Ibid.
30. Ibid., 233.
31. Ibid., 236.

32. Ibid., 238.
33. Ibid., 243.
34. Ibid., 241.
35. Fenn, *Encounters at the Heart of the World*, 290–91.
36. Kapler, *Indian Affairs*, 244.

Chapter 9

37. Witte, and Gallagher, *North American Journals of Prince Maximilian of Wied*, vol. 2.
38. Ibid., 3:207.

Chapter 10

39. Timbrook, *Inculpatory Evidence*, 44.
40. Ibid., 112.
41. Fenn, *Encounters at the Heart of the World*, 316.
42. Barbour, *Fort Union and the Upper Missouri Fur Trade*, 136.
43. Chardon, *Chardon's Journal*, 124–25.
44. Fenn, *Encounters at the Heart of the World*, 325.
45. Casler, *Steamboats of the Fort Union Fur Trade*.

Chapter 11

46. Lass, *Navigating the Missouri*, 101n.
47. Ibid., 257
48. Ibid., 77–94
49. Chittenden, *History of Early Steamboat Navigation*, 182.
50. Ibid., 187.
51. Letellier, *Louis Dace Letellier*, 11–12.

Chapter 12

52. Paul, *Blue Water Creel and the First Sioux War, 1854–56*, 148.
53. Letellier, *Louis Dace Letellier*, 15–16.

Chapter 13

54. National Park Service, Yankton Sioux Treaty Monument website https://www.nps.gov/mnrr/learn/historyculture/yankton-sioux-treaty-monument.htm.
55. Carley, *Dakota War of 1862*, 6.
56. Ibid., 11.
57. Beck, *Columns of Vengeance*, 220–36.
58. Lass, *Navigating the Missouri*, 222–23.

Chapter 14

59. *History of Steamboats on the Red River.*

Chapter 15

60. Fundingsland, *Bismarck D.T.*, 7.

Chapter 16

61. Hanson, *Conquest of the Missouri*, 240.
62. Stevenson, *Deliverance from the Little Big Horn*, 70.
63. Hanson, *Conquest of the Missouri*, 344.
64. Ibid., 345.
65. Ibid., 417.

Chapter 17

66. *Bismarck Tribune*, November 4, 1878.

Chapter 19

67. Lass, *Navigating the Missouri*, 336.
68. Ibid., 337.

69. Hanson, *Conquest of the Missouri*, 429.
70. *Bismarck Tribune*, January 28, 1938.
71. Naugle, "Minnie H Was Product of Captain E.E. Heerman's Will."
72. Robinson, *History of North Dakota*, vii.

Epilogue

73. Chittenden, *History of Early Steamboat Navigation*, 355.

BIBLIOGRAPHY

Atkinson, Henry. *Wheel Boats on the Missouri: The Journals and Documents of the Atkinson-O'Fallon Expedition, 1824–26.* Edited by Richard E. Jensen and James S. Hutchins. Helena: Montana Historical Society Press, 2001.

Barbour, Barton H. *Fort Union and the Upper Missouri Fur Trade.* Norman: University of Oklahoma Press, 2001.

Bates, Frederick. Letter to George Rogers Clark, December 1897. Bates Family Papers. Vol. 2. Missouri Historical Society, St. Louis.

Beck, Paul N. *Columns of Vengeance: Soldiers, Sioux, and the Punitive Expeditions 1863–1864.* Norman: University of Oklahoma Press, 2013.

Carley, Kenneth. *The Dakota War of 1862.* St. Paul: Minnesota Historical Society Press, 1976.

Casler, Michael M. *Steamboats of the Fort Union Fur Trade: An Illustrated Listing of Steamboats on the Upper Missouri River, 1831–1867.* Williston, ND: Fort Union Association, 1999.

Chardon, F.A. *Chardon's Journal at Fort Clark 1834–1839.* Lincoln: University of Nebraska Press, 1997.

Chittenden, Hiram Martin. *The American Fur Trade of the Far West.* Vols. 1 and 2. Lincoln: University of Nebraska Press, 1986.

———. *History of Early Steamboat Navigation: Life and Adventures of Joseph La Barge.* New York: Harpers, 1903.

Denig, Edwin Thompson. *The Assiniboine.* Norman: University of Oklahoma Press, 2000.

Douglas, Walter B. *Manuel Lisa*. New York: Argosy-Antiquarian, 1964.

Fenn, Elizabeth A. *Encounters at the Heart of the World: A History of the Mandan People*. New York: Hill and Wang, 2014.

Fundingsland, Kim. *Bismarck D.T.* Minot, ND: Niess Impressions, 2009.

Fur Trade Symposium, Indians and Traders: Entrepreneurs of the Upper Missouri. Williston, ND: Fort Union Association, 2000.

Goetsmann, William H., and Glyndwr Williams. *Atlas of North American Exploration: From the Norse Voyages to the Race to the Pole*. Norman: University of Oklahoma Press, 1992.

GreatRiverRoad.com. "Visitors Guide to the Edward 'Ted' and Pat Jones Confluence Point State Park." http://www.greatriverroad.com/stcharles/jonespark.htm.

Hanson, Joseph Mills. *The Conquest of the Missouri*. Mechanicsburg, PA: Stackpole Books, 2003.

Hart, Henry C. *The Dark Missouri*. Madison: University of Wisconsin Press, 1957.

Heidenreich, Virginia I. *The Fur Trade in North Dakota*. Bismarck: State Historical Society of North Dakota, 1990.

Hennessy, W.B. *History of North Dakota*. Bismarck, ND: Bismarck Tribune Publishing, 1910.

Herriot, Marion H. "Steamboat Transportation on the Red River." *Minnesota History Magazine* 21 (1940): 245–79.

"History of Steamboats on the Red River." Flier by the River Keepers, Fargo, 2015.

Hunter, Louis C. *Steamboats on the Western Rivers*. New York: Dover Publications, 1993.

Jackson, Donald C. *Letters of the Lewis and Clark Expedition with Related Documents 1783–1854*. Urbana: University of Illinois Press, 1978.

Jenkinson, Clay S. *A Vast and Open Plain: Writings of the Lewis and Clark Expedition in North Dakota*. Bismarck: State Historical Society of North Dakota, 2003.

Kappler, Charles J., ed. *Indian Affairs: Laws and Treaties*. Vol. 2, *Treaties*. Washington, D.C.: Government Printing Office, 1904 (from digital.library.okstate.edu).

Lass, William E. *Navigating the Missouri: Steamboating on Nature's Highway, 1819–1935*. Norman, OK: Arthur H. Clark Company, 2008.

Letellier, Louis Dace. *Louis Dace Letellier: Adventures on the Upper Missouri*. Williston, ND: Fort Union Association, 2002.

Luttig, John C. *Journal of a Fur-Trading Expedition on the Upper Missouri, 1812–1813*. Edited by Stella Drumm. St. Louis: Missouri Historical Society, 1920.

Naugle, Heerman J. "Minnie H Was Product of Captain E.E. Heerman's Will." Reprinted in the *Benson County (Minnewauken, ND) Farmers Press*, May 3, 1995.

Nelson, Bruce. *Land of the Dacotahs*. Lincoln: University of Nebraska Press, 1964.

Nester, William R. *The Arikara War: The First Plains Indian War, 1823*. Missoula, MT: Mountain Press Publishing, 2001.

Oglesby, Roger Edward. *Manuel Lisa and the Opening of the Missouri Fur Trade*. Norman: University of Oklahoma Press, 1963.

O'Neil, Paul. *The Rivermen*. New York: Time-Life Books, 1977.

Paul, R. Eli. *Blue Water Creel and the First Sioux War, 1854–56*. Norman: University of Oklahoma Press, 2004.

Potter, Tracy. *Sheheke: Mandan Indian Diplomat*. Helena, MT: Farcountry Press and Fort Mandan Press, 2003.

Robinson, Elwyn B. *History of North Dakota*. Lincoln: University of Nebraska Press, 1966.

Stevenson, Joan Nabseth. *Deliverance from the Little Big Horn: Doctor Henry Porter and Custer's Seventh Cavalry*. Norman: University of Oklahoma Press, 2012.

Timbrook, Mark J. *Inculpatory Evidence: A Reexamination of the High Plains Smallpox Epidemic of 1837 with an emphasis on the Mandan*. Minot, ND: Niess Impression, 2009.

Tweton, D. Jerome. "William Jayne: First Governor of Dakota Territory." *On Second Thought*, the journal of the North Dakota Humanities Council, Fall 2012.

Vestal, Stanley. *The Missouri*. Lincoln: University of Nebraska Press Bison Books, 1996.

Wikipedia footnote to Aeliopile. "De Architectura." Chapter 6 (paragraph 2) in *Ten Books on Architecture* by Vitruvius (first century BC). https://en.wikipedia.org/wiki/Aeolipile.

———. "Section 50: The Steam Engine." In *Hero*, written at Alexandria, Pneumatica, translated from the original Greek by Bennet Woodcroft, professor of Machinery in University College London. Reprint of first century BC original, London: Taylor Walton and Maberly, 1851. Retrieved on July 3, 2009.

Wilkins, Robert. "Alexander McKenzie and the Politics of Bossism." In *The North Dakota Political Tradition*, edited by Thomas W. Howard, 3–39. Ames: Iowa State University Press, 1981. https://en.wikipedia.org/wiki/Aeolipile.

Wischmann, Lesley. *Frontier Diplomats: The Life and Times of Alexander Culbertson and Natoyist Siskina'*. Spokane, WA: Arthur H. Clark Company, 2000.

Witte, Stephen S., and Marsha V. Gallagher, eds. *The North American Journals of Prince Maximilian of Wied*. Vol. 3. Norman: University of Oklahoma Press, 2012.

———. *The North American Journals of Prince Maximilian of Wied*. Vol. 2. Norman: University of Oklahoma Press, 2010.

Wood, Raymond W., and Thomas D. Thiessen. *Early Fur Trade on the Northern Plains*. Norman: University of Oklahoma Press, 1985.

INDEX

ABOUT THE AUTHOR

Tracy Potter writes about northern plains history in Bismarck, North Dakota, with particular interest in early relations between native peoples and people from Europe. He is the author of *Sheheke: Mandan Indian Diplomat, the Story of White Coyote, Thomas Jefferson and Lewis and Clark*. Potter retired in 2015 from a career in heritage tourism with the State of North Dakota and the Fort Abraham Lincoln Foundation, where he served as executive director and editor/ writer of the *Past Times*, a quarterly historical tabloid. He served in the North Dakota State Senate and was the Democratic-NPL nominee for the U.S. Senate in 2010. A graduate of the University of North Dakota, Potter is married to Laura Anhalt, with whom he travels widely in retirement.

Visit us at
www.historypress.net

This title is also available as an e-book